THE SPARK PLUG

An Adventure and Life Ignited by Jesus

Stephen John Oswald Jr.

ISBN: 979-8-89316-734-4 - eBook
ISBN: 979-8-89316-735-1 - Paperback
ISBN: 979-8-89316-736-8 - Hardcover

THIS BOOK IS DEDICATED TO:

Mom, Dad, Jacqlyn, and Ali. Thank you for your constant love and encouragement through every crazy idea on this roller coaster I call life. Thank you for always being there, no matter what.

Every person who helped me with this trip through finances, prayer, encouragement, or literally letting me stay in your home. This trip wouldn't have happened without you.

My niece and nephews. You can do anything you set your mind to. With God by your side, anything is possible— even if it is scary and you feel completely unqualified.

Anyone reading this who is struggling or without hope. I've been there. Multiple times. There is hope. You can get through this. Jesus loves you and has real plans for your life. You are so loved.

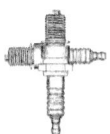

CONTENTS

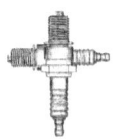

I'M NOT A WRITER

Have you ever felt that God is calling you to do something in your life? That he has put something on your heart and wants you to move forward with courageous faith and obedience in whatever this "calling" may be? It might feel scary, hard, challenging, uncomfortable. Can you relate?

I can, because…I'm not a writer. There are so many people out there that actually are writers. They went to school and studied grammar, the English language (among others probably), and actually how to write. They are the ones who are supposed to be writing.

Not me. I'm not a writer, but at a worship night over two years ago, I felt God telling me to write a book. After sharing with multiple people what the Lord had put on my heart, I naturally… took zero action and let life take over.

Months later, I woke up in the middle of the night with nothing in my mind but a book title: *The Spark Plug*. Another sign from God to be a writer. The outline for this book took maybe twelve hours to build, but with all of life's distractions, the book itself took me three years to create.

I'm really, *really* not a writer—but fortunately, I'm in good company. Moses wasn't a speaker. David wasn't big and strong. The first disciples weren't in ministry. I'm definitely not a writer, but

God is a painter. The painter of painters. He works all for his good. He tells us not to be afraid 365 times in the Bible.

And so, as an act of obedience to what I believe God is calling me to, for now, I guess I *am* a writer. I pray that the painter, the creator, the father, is the true author of this book, as he is in all of our lives.

THE SPARK PLUG

I find road trips parallel life. Not just any road trip—I'm talking about the long, extensive trips, the ones where you are wide-eyed, glued to the window 90 percent of the time with child-like amusement (when not trying to cat nap). The trips of pure adventure.

Road trips involve paths with many twists and turns, foggy roads that seem to lead into unknown lands, disastrous storms, and surreal sights. *Those* are the trips that are much like life.

One key component of a successful road trip is a functioning vehicle. All vehicles need a working engine. There is something so tiny that keeps the whole engine, and therefore the whole car, running: *The Spark Plug.* Found in an article from *Christian Brothers Automotive (2019)*: The spark plug supplies the spark that ignites the air/fuel mixture, creating the explosion which makes your engine produce power.

I don't know much about cars, but that sounds pretty essential.

During my four month, 48-state road trip, staying in people's homes I met on TikTok and adventuring with them, I realized my engine could not have made it through such an adventure without a spark plug. Just like my car, I also need a spark plug—my *Spark Plug* keeps me going through the highs of joy, the lows of feeling lost and confused, the storms, the sunshine and rainbows, and every single turn I take. My *Spark Plug* is Jesus, and that is only solidified through the amazing stories and adventures I have to tell.

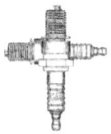

THE JOURNEY

S o, I traveled the country—well, most of it. I packed my bags at the end of May and did not return home until early September. I spent time with complete strangers and slept in their homes anywhere from one to seven days. Oh yeah, and I met the majority of these people on TikTok. How did that come to be?

The true journey began on August 30, 2020, the morning I ran a half marathon…and got baptized. This was not planned. After 24 years of living, a lifetime of searching and seeking worldly fulfillment, five years of my sister nudging me to go up and get "dunked," I did it. The only difference this Sunday? The nudge wasn't from my sister. The nudge was there, alright—maybe more than ever—but not from her. It was from him. God, Jesus, the Holy Spirit. However you refer to him, he was there.

He was telling me that after years and years of believing that baseball, girls, money, lust, comparison, and all the other stuff would fulfill me, there was only one true answer. He was telling me it didn't matter that I had let him down in my own eyes, because he had already forgiven me. He forgave me before any of it even happened. And that is a glimpse into the gospel of the real *Spark Plug*, the man I call Jesus Christ.

So *that* is where the journey begins, but it is nowhere near its ending. It is where the journey starts, because it is the moment God gave me something new: confidence. And joy. And a supernatural desire to get out of my comfort zone and live my life to the fullest. He gave me the ability to truly just be myself. He gave me a new sense of adventure to explore his creation, a new level of faith, and new fearlessness. He gave me the best gift I have ever received: a new life, ignited by *The Spark Plug*.

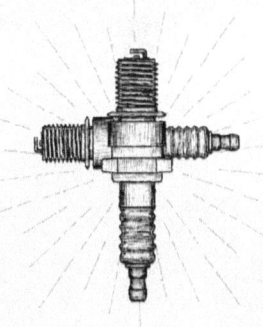

JOY

December 12, 2020 - South Dakota
165 days prior to the road trip

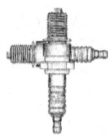

"**B**ut the holy spirit produces this kind of fruit in our lives: love, joy, peace, patience, kindness, goodness, faithfulness, gentleness, and self-control. There is no law against these things!" (Galatians 5:22-23, NLT).

I believe one of the biggest reasons I had the faith to go on this trip was Joy. That amazing "fruit" from Galatians 5 had a role in all of this, but that's not what I'm talking about. My Joy in this story is a person.

October 14, 2020, I posted a compilation on TikTok of me worshiping God, dancing goofily, jumping out of an airplane, skateboarding, and doing several other fun activities. My voiceover was all about how I was in search of a wedding date. Truthfully, this was more of a joke than anything. If I had left it up for a few hours and it sat there with minimal interactions, I probably would've deleted it out of insecurity.

But that's not what happened.

My good friend Katlyn and I had early dinner plans. When I got home and checked my TikTok, I instantly knew I would *not* be deleting the post.

Thousands of people had already seen, liked, and commented on the video. The next days were a whirlwind of direct messages, new followers, and comments across all my social media accounts. Although I never planned on this post actually leading to a wedding date, I had no other choice than to pursue a date out of the thousands of women who were begging to fly to South Dakota for a weekend to be my date. This was both weird and awesome. Naturally, the next step was to screen as many profiles as possible.

I was still at the beginning of my faith journey, having been baptized a month and a half prior, so the requirements for my date were simple: attractive and Christian. At the time, I thought, what else was there? After lengthy research, I narrowed it down to six amazing people who I FaceTimed for at least one hour each. One of them was a former New York Yankee manager's granddaughter, which is pretty cool, now that I look back on it. But man, in the end, the choice was simple. Joy.

I fell for Joy on the spot. She was a glowing woman who embodied every princess-like quality. She loved God, and when I heard her story and felt how much she loved him, I was amazed. She and her long term boyfriend had just ended their relationship, yet she was still so full of life, love, and hope in God. I was in awe of her and her faith. It was such an easy choice. Around midnight, at the end of the phone call, I told her I was giving her the rose—she got my *Bachelor* reference—and she was my choice.

That is when I first experienced her heart. Being so young in my faith, I was still learning about God and who he was. She came back with a very wise response the next morning: she told me that she wanted me to take my time with this decision and to pray about it more. She told me that Jesus *never* rushed. He always took his time loving, praying, talking, and just being. With the intent of her giving me more time to discern this decision, she just validated my choice. I was going to fly this girl across the country to South Dakota to be my wedding date.

Over the next month or two, we FaceTimed regularly and got to know each other. She was on the west coast, so it was usually at 3 a.m. or so my time, but I didn't care—I was talking to Joy! Beautiful, amazing Joy! I didn't know what it was, but there was something about her. Now I know—she encapsulated the scripture of the light and the salt in the Gospel Matthew:

> You are the salt of the earth. But what good is salt if it has lost its flavor? Can you make it salty again? It will be thrown out and trampled underfoot as worthless.
>
> You are the light of the world—like a city on a hilltop that cannot be hidden. No one lights a lamp and then puts it under a basket. Instead, a lamp is placed on a stand, where it gives light to everyone in the house. In the same way, let your good deeds shine out for all to see, so that everyone will praise your heavenly Father. (Matthew 5:13-16, NLT)

She was salt and light. She stood out. She was different, a powerful testament to God in her life. In our conversations, she was always coming back to her faith and trust in God. Whether it was having faith through the trial of losing her job due to Covid-19 or her relationship previously ending, she was always bringing the conversation back to trusting God. She was living exactly how God calls us to, and it showed.

The FaceTimes led to a great friendship even before we met. Sure, the thoughts initially were there that this could be the love of my life, but God made it clear to us both to focus on him and just be in friendship, at first. All of that led to the night before the flight.

The night before the flight I received a FaceTime as I lay in bed, prepared to wake up feeling "sick" so I could play hooky from work and drive to Omaha to pick up Joy. During this FaceTime, she told me she was worried. She was listening to the lies. People had expressed their opinions about what we were doing. Of course, not everyone was supportive, and I guess I get it. But she was fully prepared to back out and let me fly solo to my buddies' wedding. This was where Joy taught me yet another lesson: when you have fear, anxiety, stress, or believe the lies, it is probably because the enemy doesn't want you to keep going. So what did she do? She prayed and cast her fears and anxieties before God, then boarded that plane to Omaha, Nebraska.

"Cast all your anxiety on him because he cares for you" (1 Peter 5:7, NLT).

She taught me that no matter what the anxiety is, cast it on him. If it is derived from work, future, uncertainty, loss, or fear of flying across the country to meet a stranger, cast it on him.

Knowing Joy was dealing with that last-minute fear, I was unsure of what to expect when she showed up. Of course, Joy—with all her salt and light—showed up. She was the life of the whole weekend. Every little girl at the wedding who aspired to be like Joy, multiple groomsmen, and anybody she came into contact with immediately fell in love with her.

One day she was afraid to fly to South Dakota; the next, she was dancing the night away to "Mr. Brightside," even with blistered feet (princess slipper problems). And it was all because of Jesus. Jesus in Joy.

We got back from the wedding well after midnight. I knew Joy was ready to go before then, but she let me stay, hug, and dance with my friends until the very end of the night. This girl had blistered feet, traveled across the country for two and a half days, and when we arrived at our Homewood Suites hotel, beds across the room from each other, she made sure that we read the Bible and were up bright and early at church to raise our hands to God in worship.

I think we underestimate how much Jesus can work through us. If I had never met Joy and been so inspired by her, I never would have gone on my adventure across the country. I never would have thought to post my plan on TikTok, asking strangers to host me in their respective states. If Joy hadn't flown across the country to be my wedding date, I wouldn't have had the idea to have Bailey from Nebraska start the trip off with me at my friend Blake's wedding.

Not only would this trip have never happened, but my faith wouldn't be as strong as it is today if it weren't for Joy leading me with each step in her own faith. God used her in my life to teach me to slow down, to discern, to be bold and courageous, to face fear head on, and to go *all in* on God.

He used her to teach me what it was like to find true *Joy* in him. Do not underestimate how God can use you when you are faithful to him. I advise you to take a page from my book. Next time you have a big decision, are struggling, feeling anxious, or whatever it may be, I want you to think "what would Joy do?" Which is exactly the same as "What would Jesus, *The Spark Plug,* do?

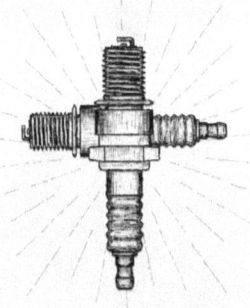

The Blessing of Barb

June 1 to June 4, 2021 - Colorado
Days 6 through 9

n the Bible—specifically, in the Gospels—Jesus tells a lot of stories. These stories, known as parables, always simplify. They make it easier to understand what Jesus is trying to communicate to us.

The story of Barb may be one of my favorites to this day. What God communicates through her is easy to understand, simple, and clear—like a parable.

But first, some backstory: when I was in college, my older sister, Ali, and her husband, Adam, lived in Colorado. I was fortunate enough to visit a couple times during the few years they resided there. Of all the trips I took, the most memorable was the time we went to Red Rocks Church.

Growing up, church didn't really "click" for me. I went to Sunday Mass until baseball took over my life, and attended other services with Ali when she lived in Chicago, but for some reason, I just didn't get it. I normally tuned out during the services, thinking about baseball or girls—two things I idolized—or other things I considered more important than God.

Way before Colorado, Ali took my family and me to church in Chicago, where she was in school. There, they worshiped. My sister, who I had known for over nineteen years to be quiet and reserved, worshiped. She ran to the front row of the huge auditorium, skipped gleefully into the very front row, and raised her hands in the air in awe and adoration of her Father. I was so confused. My other sister and I turned to each other and telepathically communicated our bewilderment. *What in the world is she doing—and what in heck is everyone else doing?* I was so unfamiliar with this behavior, and with the idea of a real, intimate, relationship with God. None of it made sense.

When Ali and Adam took me to Red Rocks Church in Colorado, I was even more confused—not because it didn't make sense, but because I went to a church service that *did* make sense. It "clicked." Even seven years later, I still remember the sermon.

It was on Ephesians 6, discussing "The Whole Armor of God." The pastor talked about someone hypothetically breaking into his house in the middle of the night, him grabbing a bat, wanting to protect his wife and kids. I don't remember how it ended, but I do remember that I *remembered* it, which I could not say about any other service I *ever* attended before that. A few years later when I was struggling in graduate school with depression, anxiety, self-worth, and much more, I started watching or listening to Red Rocks Church, weekly. God used that church to help me truly get to know Jesus. That was the initial seed, a seed planted in my soul that I had no clue about—but God did.

So, how in the world does this bring us to Barb? Fast forward to April, 2021. I had been planning this trip since fall of 2020. Colorado was one of the few states I felt very confident about, concerning the TikToker I would be staying with. Our FaceTime was great and she seemed adventurous and friendly. I had everything planned, and no worries of her backing out—until she did.

It being April, I was about one month or so from taking off on this adventure. God had made it clear to me that I needed to do this and not quit, but that story is for another chapter. When this TikToker backed out, naturally, I turned to social media for a solution. I posted on TikTok saying I needed help in Colorado and Kansas. This worked for Kansas, as I found someone willing to host me—yet, after a few days, I still had nothing from Colorado. So I dug deeper.

I remembered, during this time, that when I was searching for a wedding date, I gained at least a couple hundred new followers on Instagram. The search was on. I started scrolling through each individual follower I had gained in the last few months. I was looking for anything—an indicator in their bio of where they lived, pictures of mountains, literally anything. Then, *there it was.* I found one profile of someone who had a picture of a mountain. Jackpot! I clicked on their picture and sure enough, the location of the photo was Colorado. Colorado! I did it! I found someone who, at the very least, had been to Colorado!

After direct messaging this stranger, I received the good news: she did, in fact, live in Colorado. We set up a phone call and I could see that God had blessed me with an answered prayer...until she told me during our phone call that she didn't think it was a good idea, because she had a new boyfriend and wasn't sure about things with him. But she had a friend, and this was way up her alley!

So now the girl who had a picture of Colorado on her social media couldn't show me around, but she had a friend who could. Awesome. Time to call this friend, named—of course—Faith. Faith was very direct and told me that she would love to host me, show me around, and hang out. However, she was going to be out of town the dates I would be stopping by. But she had a friend, Barb, whom she believed would totally help me out, no question. She gave me Barb's number and I sent an introductory text.

That evening, after finding a picture of a mountain on social media, being referred by a stranger to a friend, to another friend, I received a text back from Barb.

The first text I ever received from Barb was a picture of a mountain. That's it. No message attached. Nothing but a mountain. Ten minutes after receiving a random photo of a mountain, a long paragraph came through. Discussing this lack of youthful text etiquette with my sister, she made the very clear point that the woman's name is Barb—she is most likely old. That was something I had not considered before.

Now, I had a very clear plan in mind for my Colorado visit: hang out with young hipsters who knew the vibe and would show me the ins and outs of their dope state. Barb did not fit that bill, but it was near impossible to make the case that this chain of events wasn't from God, so I had to make the phone call. Barb, who was at the dog park, had plenty of time to talk. I realized she was just as reserved and uncertain about this whole thing as I was—that is, until she asked me why I was doing this road trip.

Months prior, when I was first planning this trip, a couple cool dudes named Hunter and Caleb were showing me what it's like to walk with Jesus. They asked me how I was going to incorporate my faith on this four-month trip. After much thought, prayer, and conviction, I told them that this was a mission trip. Now, I told the same thing to Barb. I wanted to share God's story of what he had done in my life, and I wanted to glorify him. As God does, he flung the door wide open—our conversation completely changed and became so free as we both openly discussed our faith with each other.

Hmmm…It's almost like things are always better and more fruitful when God is at the center.

We were both starting to think this was meant to be when Barb mentioned that her daughter, Skylar, used to intern at the one and only Red Rocks Church. That decided it. I was going to stay just outside of Denver, Colorado with my new, sixty-something-year-old friend, Barb.

One month later, I was greeted with a hug from Barb, who came exactly as advertised on the phone: a thoughtful, intentional, hospitable, loving, and kind woman who let the Lord lead her every step. I could sit here and write about all the amazing things Barb did that week—like intentionally planning for me to have time with her daughter and her friends so I was with people my age, making sure I went to a Colorado Rockies game, and taking me on multiple beautiful hikes—but I won't. I want to speak not about the things that Barb planned, but about who she is.

Barb is a disciple. She is an advocate for the kingdom of God and his son, Jesus, and the desire to see that kingdom grow and flourish here on earth. Barb is a gift from God, someone from whom the Holy Spirit flows out of and into others.

Until this point in my life, I don't think I had met anyone quite like Barb. She was so intentional in her faith and her relationship with God. It was modeled by her actions, shown by her words, and made clear by her heart.

Back on our first phone call, she told me all about a young man she'd met whom she was praying for and sharing Jesus with.

My first morning with her, before we went on a hike, she was clear that she was spending time with God in scripture and in prayer.

On the drive to our hike, she asked questions that led to me sharing God's story of my life—my testimony.

Every hike, lunch, and dinner came with intentional conversations about life, living, and God. Not to mention she covered every meal to lessen the financial burden on me.

Barb gifted me a sheet of paper full of scripture that correlated to who God says you are, which I was later able to gift to someone else.

Every part of my stay with Barb and her family was intentional, but the most intentional moment would be when Barb directed Skylar and her friends, Kate, John, and Isaac, to take me along with them to a young adults' night at Red Rocks Church. I was finally able to go back to the place where God had started it all, where that original seed had been planted.

Can we just take a second to be in awe of God? God is the God of full circles. God is the God of puzzles. He knows what the beautiful puzzle looks like when it is finished, while we only have knowledge of a few pieces attached to each other. To my future self, and whoever else may read this, God is in control of the puzzle and, when complete, it is a masterpiece.

All the hardships, valleys, blessings, and peaks are part of the puzzle. The most beautiful part is trusting in the hands of the puzzle maker. He'll put you in a church service in Colorado, changing your perspective on him and faith, then bring you back years later after going through so many ups and downs and changing your whole life to show you the puzzle's beautiful completion.

So, although this chapter is about Barb, we must remember that this book as a whole is really about God and *The Spark Plug* that he is. The puzzle of heaven is so beautiful, and the pieces along the way are our beautiful journey toward joining him there. Focus on the puzzle maker, not the puzzle pieces.

That puzzle maker brought me Barb, who could have hosted me for five days and never talked to me again—but like I said, she is a disciple. The day I left for Utah, Barb called me on my long drive. When I left Utah for Idaho, Barb called me. When I left Idaho for Montana, Barb called me. Barb called me during every single drive

I made over the next four months—and she didn't just call me; she intentionally checked in with me, sent me sermons, and prayed for me. She taught me and discipled me. I arrived home from this trip in September of 2021, and Barb still reaches out multiple times throughout the year as I write this book in 2024.

I compared the story of Barb to a parable, saying it was easy to understand, simple, and clear. The story of Barb is simple. As Jesus poured into his disciples with love, grace, mercy, knowledge, and wisdom, while walking alongside them, so does Barb.

If you are ever stuck or lost in the puzzle, thinking nothing makes sense, thinking that your plan is better than God's, I urge you to trust him and give him control. His final solution is masterful, and he just might bless you with a Barb.

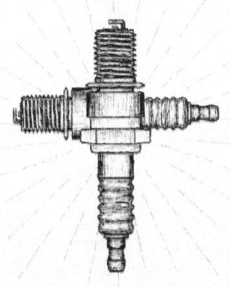

PLANS
UNRAVELED

July 9 to July 12, 2021 - New Mexico
Days 44 through 47

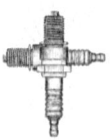

When I was in middle school, my uncle Greg had an astonishingly huge Christamas gift waiting under the tree that was begging to be opened by his girlfriend. The gift was taller and wider than me, well above five feet. I was excited about this gift, and it wasn't even mine! After patiently waiting through the childrens' gifts, his future fiancé finally opened hers as our whole family waited in anticipation. What she found inside was a surprise to all of us.

It was another box, perfectly wrapped, just slightly smaller than the outer box. She opened this box to find another box, and another box, and another box, until she opened the tiniest of presents. I think it was jewelry. He might have even proposed at that moment. I really don't remember, because I was just so mesmerized by the concept of twenty-five boxes wrapped as one. Every gift that was opened or unraveled led to another gift, all leading to the ultimate gift.

I think God kind of works this way with his plans. Some would call them his will or calling for our lives. God's plan, will, or calling for our lives slowly unravels and unravels, until we reach the ultimate gift: heaven. That said, there are a lot of plans to be unraveled while we are on this earth before we reach heaven.

If God knows the "final puzzle" or the "ultimate gift" and knows exactly how we get there, then why can't we know, too?

"And we know that God causes everything to work together for the good of those who love God and are called according to his purpose for them" (Romans 8:28, NLT).

We humans often think we know what is best for our lives, exactly what we need, when we need it, and how it will come to us. We think we know best, but more often than not, life proves us wrong. Truthfully, we do not know best. However, we are so lucky because the creator of the universe and every one of us *does* know exactly what is best, according to his purpose.

So, why can't we know how the puzzle pieces fit, or why can't we have the final gift now? Because God knows so much better than we do. Because God wants to teach us patience, trust, and obedience, among many other things, all while increasing our faith in him.

Kate is an unraveled plan that God had for my life and for this trip. While frantically trying to figure out where and with whom I would be staying in Kansas and Colorado, I pushed to the back of my mind the fact that many other people from many other states were *also* backing out or ghosting me.

God's plan in Colorado was for me to meet Barb's daughter's friend, Kate. (I know, it sounds like I'm talking about something distant, like my friend's cousin's fish's veterinarian's step-daughter's cousin, twice removed, but truth can be stranger than fiction. You can't make this stuff up—only God can.)

Kate and I were able to spend a day together when she took me on a short trip to the town of Boulder, Colorado. We drove to the top of a mountain with one of the most insane views I have ever seen, a view that makes you jealous of the birds and their freedom to soar wherever they like. We strolled through the quaint, hipster town before broadening my palette with spicy Indian food. Kate's ability to listen and be present was one of her gifts. As she showed me around on our stroll, we were able to connect on a deeper level while sharing our testimonies of how God has worked in our lives. Just like with Barb, this brought us to a deeper level of connection and friendship, all in one day! That's what God does when he is in the center: he ignites something, kind of like a *Spark Plug*.

I knew Kate and I would be lifelong friends when we blasted "Unwritten" by Natasha Bedingfield, windows down at a very long red light—many eyes were glued on us from nearby cars. Spending the next few days with other young people—reading Psalms with Skylar before she went to work, connecting with John as he took me through a 6 a.m. lift, and being able to pray with Kate in the Sonic parking lot—was perfect. Upon leaving Colorado, I was very hopeful to see all these people again soon. I just didn't know how soon.

Five hours later, I was driving to Utah and still had hours left on the drive. So, I figured, why not call my new friend Kate? Kate was nannying and slightly distracted by the boys she was watching at the lake, but she was still "there." To find a friend who is present and able to be there, even though they're busy, is a true gift. Knowing this friendship was such a gift from God, we immediately discussed when we could meet again. The stars aligned perfectly when Kate—knowing that I had no one to stay with me a month later in New Mexico—told me that she had once been to Santa Fe and would love to go back.

Now, none of this would have happened if I had stayed with my original contact in Colorado. None of this would have ever happened if I decided not to stay with Barb because she was "too old"—not trusting God and not being obedient to him. This was so clearly God's plan, and none of it was what I expected. In fact, it was better. It was all him; I just had to *wait*, *trust*, and *follow*.

So, here's what he cooked up. He brought me to Colorado and gifted me Barb, which was already an amazing story—but through being patient, trusting him, and being obedient to his plan, he also brought me Kate, the next marvelous gift.

About a month later, after I had worked my way down the west coast, Kate and I reconnected in the middle of thousands of evergreens, in Santa Fe, New Mexico.

The best part of our weekend together was the unpredictability. We determined beforehand that each of us would plan a day in New Mexico, with one twist—we wouldn't tell each other what we had planned. The element of surprise and the anticipation of the unknown is a beautiful thing.

On the first night, while driving to get groceries, we saw the most amazing sunset I have ever seen. We had to pull over for a photoshoot to capture the stunning sight. We had a mission to get to the store, buy our donuts, and get back without stopping, but God had other plans.

Kate planned the first day, which—I will not lie—was much more structured than mine. Kate had done her research and had the day all worked out. After donuts, we set out for Day One of adventuring. We pulled into the parking lot of a place called Meow Wolf. This was one of the quirkiest, coolest, and most interesting places I've ever been. It was like a trip to a fantasy world, where you forget you're not really in that time and place. After hours of continuous stimulation from Meow Wolf, we explored downtown Santa Fe and rounded out the evening at a restaurant that once again pushed me out of my palate's comfort zone.

After dinner, there was another gorgeous sunset. We quickly searched out the closest lookout point and found another breathtaking view. The sunset looked mere miles away, descending onto the mountains, while we and twenty other strangers saw all of this at the foot of a cross overlooking Santa Fe. Wow. The amazing part about Kate is that she had a plan, but she was so okay with it changing on a whim. She knew that things could end up even better than planned.

My Day Two plan wasn't very planned. I woke up with absolutely nothing decided. To avoid stressing out my friend, I left that part out. It felt like a good day for a hike, so that's what we did. We followed each other up a mountain while having life-giving conversations and flinching every time I mistook a lizard for a snake. After the long hike, I had no further plans, but what better idea than to fill our stomachs? I acted like I knew exactly where I was going until I pulled into a random, fast food Mexican Restaurant. We then did something I had never done before: we didn't even read the menu. I pulled up to the drive-through and said, "We will have the 1, 5, 7, and throw in some desserts, too."

We ended up driving to a local soccer field to have our feast. We slowed down and watched kids play catch, adults pepper a volleyball, and filled up our stomachs because I ordered way too much food. We then went back to our lodgings and I told Kate I had plans, but really I just went into goofy mode. I put on my cowboy hat, an unbuttoned flannel, and told her to follow me on a hike in our "backyard" full of thousands of trees. Basically, she just witnessed me making a fool of myself and trying to be entertaining for twenty minutes, but it was fun. It was *all unplanned*, but man was it good.

Day One, Kate knew the plan and I didn't. Day Two, neither of us knew the plan. But both times, we were patient to see what was to come, we were trusting of each other, and we were obedient or willing to follow each other with faith in the other's plan.

On a deeper level, there are two people in history who were extremely patient, trusting, and obedient to God's plan for their lives, even when it was extremely difficult. Jesus lived an incredible life, doing the most humble and vulnerable thing he could do: he became a man and lived a life where he loved, healed, and poured out so much, all the while being hated, mocked, and ultimately suffering death on the cross for us. Jesus had a calling for his life, and God had a master plan for it. The calling of Jesus's life was to share God with everyone, and to love everyone, even if they weren't pleasant or helpful to him. The plans were ultimately for us and for the growth of God's kingdom.

The night before Jesus was betrayed and crucified, dying a painful, undeserving death, he prayed on the Mount of Olives.

> "Father, if you are willing, please take this cup of suffering away from me. Yet, I want your will to be done, not mine." Then an angel from heaven appeared and strengthened him. He prayed more fervently and he was in such agony of spirit that his sweat fell to the ground like great drops of blood. (Luke 22:42-44, NLT)

Jesus knew this was going to happen. He knew throughout his life that he would be the ultimate sacrifice for us. He knew the true blessing would be in heaven. He could have easily said, "I'm out," and run off to live his own life. He had so much wisdom and knowledge. He could have become rich, been loved by all, and could have lived his own life, but he knew God's will was greater. Although his ultimate gift would come after resurrection, he was patient, trusting, and obedient to his father.

Paul's story is just as amazing. Paul was literally killing the Lord's followers. Let me say that again: he wanted to murder God's followers, but God had other plans! Paul had an encounter with God, and that's all The *Spark Plug* he needed to change his whole life. Paul completely changed his life and gave up everything for God. He boldly proclaimed his faith everywhere he went. He also faced persecution and penalties. Whether it was threats of prison or death, he didn't care. As Paul pressed on his journey, many told him to stop and not go on to Jerusalem, as he would face jail or death.

"But he said, 'Why all this weeping? You are breaking my heart! I am ready to not only be jailed at Jerusalem but even to die for the sake of the Lord Jesus'" (Acts 21:13, NLT).

Paul was only in this position because he followed God's plan for his life. God completely changed his life overnight, literally, but Paul didn't question God. Instead, he changed everything about himself and gave it all to God, being patient, trusting, and obedient to him.

"Don't store up treasures here on earth, where moths eat them and rust destroys them, and where thieves break in and steal. Store your treasures in heaven, where moths and rust cannot destroy, and thieves do not break in and steal. Wherever your treasure is, there the desires of your heart will also be" (Matthew 6:19-21, NLT).

At the beginning of this chapter, I mentioned that people group God's "plans," "will," or "calling" together as one. This isn't quite right. In truth, the plans he has are different for every single one of us, but we all have the *same* calling, will, or purpose. Last year, a friend told me it was so great I knew my purpose—to share Jesus and try to love like him—and they wished they knew theirs.

Well, I believe Jesus and Paul taught us what *all* of our purposes are: to follow the plans God has for our lives, just like they did. As each plan unraveled, and they lived out their calling of sharing God, they were one step closer to the final gift: the treasure of heaven. God has a different plan for each of our lives, but we are all called to have faith, like Jesus and Paul—and to share it. As each plan is unraveled, we may learn that some may be true blessings and some may be extreme trials, but they all lead to the final, true gift.

We may not know each puzzle piece, each unopened present, or the unknown plan along the way, but I think that's a good thing. It allows us to wait in excitement and anticipation, with faith in the one who knows the plan. Like my uncle's Christmas present, each gift unwrapped is beautiful and exciting, no matter the outcome, and they are always leading to the final gift, which is the biggest blessing ever. So, whether it's a road trip, career, relationship, or just the day ahead, be patient, be trustful, be obedient, and let your faith grow in him.

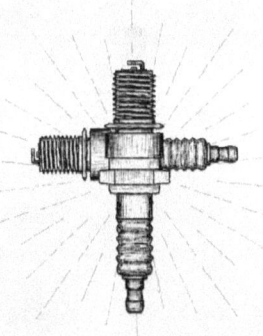

SHAKE-A-DAY

March 19, 2021 - South Dakota
69 days prior to the road trip

*Y*our dreams are too small if they are possible without divine intervention from God. I read something along those lines in a book written by Mark Batterson, *In A Pit With A Lion On A Snowy Day.*

I didn't realize how impossible of a dream this trip would be alone, but God made it clear: I needed him to complete this epic trek.

The beginning stages were fun and exciting, as most new adventures are. I had FaceTimed about sixty people in three weeks. I woke up, went to work, then FaceTimed until as late as 1 a.m. for my west coasters, and then did it all over again, every night, for three weeks straight. Each FaceTime led to a stranger committing to house me about nine months down the road. I had it all figured out. Where I was going to stay, when I was going to be at each location, and who I was going to stay with. It was time to sit back and relax until May, when the trip began…or so I thought.

As the page turned to the new year of 2021, I realized some of these people whom I was relying on maybe weren't so reliable. Many had stopped responding, leading to slight discouragement and fear of this trip falling apart. For the time being, I decided these people were just busy during the holiday season and all was going to work out swell.

At a similar time, January 2021, I decided I was going to complete the "75 Hard Challenge." I would strongly recommend *not* doing this challenge while working two jobs and living in snowy South Dakota during the wintertime. Between working out two times a day (one outdoors), drinking a gallon of water, changing my diet, and much more, I also had to read ten pages of a book everyday.

Now, I wasn't much of a reader. The last time I read so much was in third grade, when they awarded me "Accelerated Reader" points for reading difficult books. That's when it was fun. Nonetheless, I had to read something, so my first step was to make a selection.

Not being a huge reader, I had no clue what book to hop into. Luckily, I was living at my sister's place, so I ventured to her and her husband's "reading room." What I found in the reading room was *In A Pit With A Lion On A Snowy Day*. The cover looked cool, and so naturally, I was intrigued.

This book, which I picked out of hundreds at random, was exactly what I needed. As I read, I realized it was God telling me that although I had slight discouragement, this trip still needed to happen. Sometimes God speaks to us or directs us, and we may not even know it. His works aren't always obvious, but his timing is always perfect.

While God was encouraging me through this book to dream big and "go for it," I was still working two jobs. My second job was fancy, eloquent, and tasteful…just kidding. Actually, I was a bartender in a small town of 2,000, working my butt off every weekend to save up money for my cross-country travels. The place was such a dive bar that it was just called "My Bar." My mom bartended there for years before I came on staff. When she said she was going to work at "my bar," I thought she literally meant "the bar that she worked at." Her bar.

STEPHEN JOHN OSWALD JR.

My Bar had a fun game (a fun game if you like being scammed out of your hard-earned money, that is): the Shake-A-Day. Commonly seen in small-town bars, the Shake-A-Day is very simple, but near impossible. Remember that: *near impossible.*

The rules are as follows: you pay one dollar to shake five dice in a cup. You can only shake one time per day. If you match three dice when you roll them, you get another roll; match four dice and you win a free drink; match all five dice, and you win 80 percent of the pot (so the remaining 20 percent can be saved to start the the next pot and fuel gambling addictions—which I do not condone).

Come late March, I wasn't quite done with the 75 Hard Challenge, but I had finished the book that told me my dreams were only big enough if I *needed* God for them to be possible. Like most humans, reading the book was amazing, but retaining and remembering what I read two months later, when I needed the encouragement again, was not so easy.

It was time to face the facts: people were backing out of this trip and ghosting me. My hours and hours of FaceTime investments were all proving to be a waste of time, as half of them told me they couldn't help me anymore or just flat out would not respond. My trip was only a few months away, but I was completely discouraged. I started to believe the lies that this trip was a stupid idea and that I should give up. I failed to remember one important thing: the lies are not from God, and when you are trying to do something big with God in it, the enemy is going to try to stop you. But boy, do I have good news for you: Jesus, *The Spark Plug,* always wins.

I started the Friday night shift at My Bar super discouraged. A kind gentleman named Jeff laid a dollar in front of me and said, "I want you to play the Shake-A-Day." Jeff was known to me as the really kind guy who loved cheap beer and good conversation, and always tipped really well. So when he told me he would rather have me play his dollar on a game that is near *impossible* to win rather than keep the dollar as a tip, I wasn't exactly ecstatic. Nonetheless I let my five dice spew out of the cup to see that I had matched four out of five dice. I *almost* achieved the near impossible and won the pot of over one-thousand dollars—but instead, I won a free liquid ice energy drink to propel me through the remainder of my shift. I couldn't have been more grateful.

Fast forward a week later, and Jeff, drinking his Hamm's, laid down another dollar asking when I was going to "shake." At this point, after almost winning the week before, I was fully on board. You know what they say, "Scared money don't make money." I told Jeff I was ready to roll right then and there. As I went back to the register to put my gifted dollar bill in, I picked up my cross necklace and said, "God, if I win this money, I will put it all toward my road trip where I am going to try to glorify you in everything I do. I also will give ten percent to your Kingdom." That was it. I didn't ask to win, but told God, if this is your will, here's what I'm going to do.

I turned back to the bar and went right in front of my boss, Shelly the owner, so she could witness the shake. As I did this, I had the most calming feeling. Like, I was in a room full of people, but I was the only one who knew what was about to happen.

My boss Shelly laid down a dollar and said, "Here, I'll go after you."

I so softly, playfully, and confidently responded, "Shelly, you're not going to want to roll after me." I grabbed my cross for everyone to see, blew hot air on the dice, cupped it with both hands, and shook it dramatically until Shelly urged me to just roll the dang thing.

There is no such thing as coincidences. Five 3s. All the same number—a holy number, at that. The Father. The Son. The Holy Spirit. I didn't win another roll, I didn't win a free drink—I had just won over 2,000 dollars. Emphatically throwing our hands up in the air, Jeff and I couldn't believe it. No one could. The bartender, who normally takes all of our money, just won the pot right in front of our eyes and is bringing it home to stash in his shoebox—I'm sure the customers thought exactly that.

Encouragement. I was at a point of almost giving up on my God-sized dream. I was about to throw in the towel and not travel the United States sharing my faith in Jesus. *But,* God said, "No, son, you are going on this trip, whether you like it or not." The Shake-A-Day win was all I needed to make me completely ecstatic for the coming May. I was thrilled, because I just received confirmation from the living God that he wanted me to do this! And if this was God's plan, nothing was going to stop it.

So what are the odds? That is a question we hear a lot, sometimes referring to our God-sized dreams (our dreams that are only possible with God). Well, I was intrigued to find out what the odds of rolling five dice the same number were on one roll. Turns out, they weren't very good. To be exact, they were .08 percent. That's not only less than 1 percent—that's *less than one-tenth of 1 percent.* How amazing is that? It was nearly *impossible,* but guess what? *Nothing,* and I mean absolutely *nothing* is impossible with God.

Has God placed a dream on your heart? A dream so big, so daunting, so challenging that it seems so much easier to just be afraid and not take a step toward that dream? A dream that is challenging and maybe even impossible to do on your own? A dream that, when it is achieved, will only bring glory to God because you can tell everyone he is the one who brought you through it? A dream that the devil hates? A dream like sharing your faith on a cross-country road trip or writing a book about God's part in that trip? That is what I call a God-sized dream, and that is how big God calls you to dream.

If that is not you right now, know that it can be. In fact, God wants it to be. He wants you to dream so big that you *need* to rely on him, because all he wants is us and our hearts, dreams, hopes, and aspirations. He wants the good and the bad. He wants *all* of it and he wants *all* of us.

If that is you right now, you're in good company. I say, chase the dream. Take the steps, and when you feel discouraged—because you will—keep going. Keep him in the center of it; in fact, invite him into it every single day. Let him know that this dream is absolutely not possible on your own without him. He will show up, his timing will be perfect, and he will defy the odds.

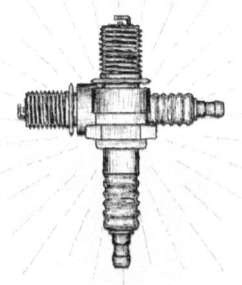

Just Pray

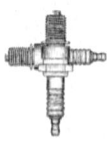

*J*ust pray.

Kind of like Nike—"just do it." Just pray.

I pray before every single chapter is written. I pray and ask God to write these chapters through me. I pray for him and the Holy Spirit in me to write. I pray that he does all the work through my heart, mind, soul, and of course, fingertips. So although my name may be on the cover, I gladly defer all credit for this book. But why? Why do I pray, and why do I invite him into everything I do?

Well because, according to the Shake-A-Day, God not only hears prayers, he also *answers* prayers. I pray because God absolutely wants and desires a relationship with us where we are in constant communication with him. Because God wants us to believe in him and his promises for us. Because God wants us to know he is there for us. Because God wants to strengthen and encourage us and those around us. Because God wants to heal us and protect us. Because God wants the absolute best for us. Because we need God. Because God is our father. Because God is a *way* better author than I am. Because...why not? What's the worst thing that could happen if you did pray? I don't think the question is, "Why do you pray?" I think the real question is, "Why on earth *wouldn't* you pray?"

Before God changed my life in 2020, I prayed…but admittedly, I didn't really understand prayer. I didn't really understand God. Up to the age of twenty-three, I prayed a lot differently than I do now.

I said the same prayer: "God, I love you. Thank you for everything you have ever done for me. Please look after my family and friends and keep them healthy. Please let my family members who have passed away know I love them and can't wait to see them again. Please bring me a wife." This was the general format, with maybe some additional requests depending on what life was bringing my way. There is nothing wrong with these things. But I said this same exact prayer every single time I prayed. I said it at the same exact time of day, and I never prayed more than once per day.

I have seen many failed relationships, as well as many successful relationships. Other than having the foundation of the relationship be God, the successful ones have had very important qualities: they communicated extremely well (daily), they were great friends, and they spent good, quality time together—among other things.

It's the same way with our father. Our *father*. Many of us have significant relationships with our parents—don't you think it's that much more important to have a real, raw, authentic relationship with your heavenly father? To be able to talk to him about anything and everything—the good, the bad, the ugly? To be able to talk to him whenever you want throughout the day, to just spend time with him—now *that* sounds like a real relationship.

Leading up to and during this trip, God helped me grow so much in my prayer life and taught me so much about himself and prayer. Here's what I learned:

PRAY OUT LOUD

October 2, 2020 - South Dakota
43 days after baptism - 237 days prior to the road trip

In May of 2020, my good friend Riley started a Bible study over Zoom due to the COVID-19 pandemic that was sweeping the nation. Riley, you may not know this, but that Bible study truly helped lead me to Jesus. Thank you, brother. At the time, I was super new to this "Bible study" stuff, and extremely scared. I didn't want to say the wrong thing or embarrass myself, because I didn't know much about the Bible at all. So, once we got to the end and he asked for prayer requests, even if I had someone in my life who desperately needed prayer, I kept my lips locked. I was afraid of what others would think. I was extremely insecure.

If you are new to your faith in Jesus, please know that you don't have to know a certain amount to be good enough, and you never have to be insecure in your faith or where you are at in your journey. All God wants is your heart. If you believe and have given him your heart, that is it. Learn from me—believe in that, and have confidence in it!

But I didn't know that yet. Back then, since I couldn't even ask others to pray something for me, I didn't know how I could ever pray out loud, even by myself.

Later that year, about a month after I had been baptized, the new men's Bible study I joined told us there was going to be a "worship night" the next week, and that we should consider going. The worship night was on a Friday evening.

At this time, I really was struggling with the fact that I was single, and I felt the strong urge to pray throughout the day. This wasn't normal for me yet; my whole life, prayer had been a nighttime routine, but as I had been learning about having a relationship with God, I realized I could talk to him whenever—so I did.

The morning of the worship night, I prayed in my car on the way to work. I prayed during my breaks at work. Then, the defining moment—I decided to go on a hike that led to my favorite spot: a hidden, secluded hill in the middle of a ski range that had not yet been found out by others. Eventually, someone moved a couch to the spot—not all good things last.

I'll never forget that Friday on that hill. I decided to get on my knees and speak to God—I mean, *actually* talk to him. I spoke to him aloud like he was my friend. I told him my hurts, my heart, my desires, my doubts. I told him everything. And it was amazing. I didn't know talking to God could be so freeing until I truly believed that he was listening and was right there.

A few hours later, I was quite unsure if I should attend the worship night, especially because I had never been to one and I wouldn't know anyone there. The enemy was trying to tell me not to go because it was Friday night, because I wouldn't know anyone, because it wasn't my scene. I believe he knew that God was going to absolutely change my life that night, and he was trying to do anything to stop it. This is a friendly reminder, *The Spark Plug* always wins.

I decided to take the chance and go to this worship night. I entered *scared, intimidated,* and *fearful,* and I left *changed, ecstatic,* and *free.* That's what God does.

On the drive there, I decided I should pray out loud again. I told God, "I feel like I'm growing in my faith and going in the right direction. I don't want to get complacent and comfortable, though. Could you speak something to me or show me something so I can stay encouraged and keep growing?"

Boy, did he answer.

I went in, even though I literally knew two people out of a hundred. One guy I had only met the week before, at Bible study. The other was my high school friend's younger brother, whom I hadn't seen in six years. The point is, I knew no one there and no one there knew me, or anything about me.

About an hour into the worship, I realized this wasn't a normal worship night. There was a man there named Josh. Josh started speaking on a microphone, and he randomly called out and said, "My brother in the blue, what's your name?"

He meant me. I was thinking, "I came here for a worship night. What the heck is going on?" I responded with, "Stephen."

This is what he said: "Everything about your life is getting ready to change, for your heart and your pursuit of God have brought you to a place of greatness—do you believe that? In the seasons of struggle when you felt like you wanted to give up, and you felt like you didn't matter, you felt like nobody cared. But God says, 'Today, I see you, son. And I count you. I count you! I count you.' When you count yourself out, God says, 'I count you.' And today, there's a fresh strength being released into your heart—are you ready for that? And the struggles—I just see it—the struggles of yesterday are being broken off of you today, and the words, curses, and the lies you have spoken against yourself are being broken off your spirit. Why? Because God's love is far greater!"

I froze. Everything that was said was true. I wanted to give up in life, I felt like I didn't matter, and I felt like no one cared about me. So much so that a year prior I journaled how I was suicidal and was only not going to get to that point because 1) My uncle had taken his life, and I know if I did it, my mom couldn't handle it, and 2) God has planned a whole life for me, and I need to see it through to see his plans come to fruition.

When Josh spoke these words over me, it didn't feel like Josh. It felt like God. It *was* God, through Josh. I was literally stuck in shock, awe, and amazement. The living God was speaking directly to me, right after I decided to speak to him earlier that day. I didn't know he could do that. I didn't know he was alive like that, but now I do, and I'll never forget. And he was right, everything about my life was getting ready to change. And now it has. God has completely changed me and my life. Wow.

For me, to pray out loud is to know that God is real and alive. It is to know that I can have a real, authentic relationship with our creator. And you can, too.

PERSPECTIVE ON PRAYER

May 25, 2021 - South Dakota
Two days prior to the road trip

A few nights before the trip, I was savoring my time with two good friends, Dianna and Julia. We were sitting in my 2010 Toyota Corolla, jamming out, just being our goofy selves. Conversation eventually landed on my foot pain. I had felt pain in my foot for weeks and was expressing my worries that it could be bothersome during the adventure ahead.

Dianna asked me a very profound question: "Have you prayed for God to heal it?"

I giggled, but then I saw the seriousness in Dianna's eyes. Straightening up, I responded that I had not prayed about it yet.

"Well, why not? Don't you believe God can heal it?"

Of course I believed he could heal my foot, but did I think he actually would? Leading up to that moment, no. I knew God was capable of anything, but I didn't actually believe he would do those things for me, so why even ask? I figured God had bigger fish to fry, and if I had a slight pain in my foot, what was the point? I could get through it, and it would heal on its own eventually.

But thank God for friends like Dianna. She was persistent that we pray for my foot, right there in my car. The funny thing about when God answers our prayers is that half the time, we don't even realize it. A few days later, about a week into my trip, I had the thought, "Wait! When did my foot stop hurting?!"

That night in the car, there was a shift in faith and a shift in my perspective of who God really was. This shift that wasn't just needed for this road trip, but for this life. My friend Dianna's faith was beautiful. My faith was limited. Deep down, I held restraints in my mind of what I thought God could and couldn't do.

It's like when Jesus cast an evil spirit out of a young boy. The boy's father said to Jesus, "The spirit often throws him into the fire or into water, trying to kill him. Have mercy on us and help us, if you can."

> "What do you mean, 'If I can?'" Jesus asked. "Anything is possible if a person believes." The father instantly cried out, "I do believe, but help me overcome my unbelief!" (Mark 9:22-24, NLT).

That's exactly what Jesus did in my life through Dianna. He helped me overcome my disbelief. He helped change my perspective of prayer. Even more, he helped change my perspective of him.

God may not answer every single prayer. He does in fact know what's best at the end of the day. But I know God will answer more prayers if we don't confine him to our small, human beliefs. *Let God be big.* Whether the prayer is big or small, let him be big. Let him decide if he should answer the prayer or not. *Believe* that he will and *know* that he can.

PRAY IN SORROW

May 30 to June 1, 2021 - Kansas
Days 4 through 6

I had an amazing two days with Carlie from Kansas. I didn't have very high expectations for Wichita, Kansas, but our adventure certainly blew those expectations away. We had a blast playing corn hole (or "bags"—let's not argue), dancing in the rain for everyone to see, throwing axes, sneaking into Wichita State's baseball field (shhh—don't tell), and having an amazing conversation about our faith and beliefs while enjoying Andy's ice cream. It couldn't have been better scripted. However, the morning of my departure for Colorado was struck with great sorrow.

Carlie was a proud mom of two tiny dogs, Sadie and Lilly. The night before I left, Lilly had started to seize. Carlie did not know whether to go to the emergency vet or what else to do. After a couple phone calls and Lilly starting to calm down, the decision was made to let it be for the night, as all signs were pointing toward a healthy pup the next morning.

Tears are what I woke up to. My dear friend Carlie had lost her beautiful friend in the middle of the night. Upon hearing my new friend cry and seeing Sadie run around, uncertain of why Lilly wouldn't play with her, I was shocked and saddened. This was one week into my trip and I was absolutely not prepared for this situation. No one ever really is. With a heavy heart, I tried my best to comfort Carlie. In reality though, I had no clue what to do. I then learned that when there isn't any answer, there is really only one answer: *pray*. I asked Carlie if I could pray for her and Lilly at that moment.

Carlie asked me that day, as I headed west, if dogs went to heaven. I told her that I really didn't know. What I did know is that life is hard. It is full of loss, grief, and pain. Most of the time it makes no sense. I also know it is easy to want to turn away from God in these moments because life just doesn't make any sense. Remember this: he is right there with you. He is grieving with you and he will not leave you. Those moments are so hard, yet they are the moments that we need him most. I urge you to pray to *The Spark Plug* in jubilation, frustration, sadness, loss, and all else. Remember, in the storm, he is still there, and wants to help us through. Keep your eyes on him.

PRAY WITH OTHERS

July 6 to July 9, 2021 - Arizona
Days 41 through 44

The first time I ever prayed out loud with someone else was with my pregnant sister, for her and her unborn baby. Today, I'm blessed to watch my nephew run around and play with not a care in the world.

Asking my sister if I could pray for her was extremely scary, but extremely worth it, because 1) she needed it, 2) it was encouraging to her, and 3) it helped grow my faith and hers. God solidified to me that we are not supposed to walk this walk alone. Praying together brings hope, encouragement, and—always—increased faith.

Just like praying with my sister, praying with new friend Shannon in Arizona brought much hope, encouragement, and increased faith—in her, and in me. Shannon was all in—as she always was. She embraced life and every adventure thrown her way. Shannon wanted to squeeze every ounce of fun out of our time together in downtown Phoenix. The country club, pedicures, a ghost town, getting kicked out from sightseeing a mountain in a restricted area, and grilling for her family with essentially no chef experience were just the tip of the iceberg.

The rest of the iceberg is what God did in Phoenix, because nothing else can amount to that.

As mentioned, the intent was for this to be a mission trip, organically sharing my faith whenever God allowed it. I realized something on this trip, though—sharing your faith isn't always easy. In fact, it can be quite hard. It can be awkward and uncomfortable, and is certainly not always organic.

Early on in the trip, I was so focused on God, and he was showing himself so much, that it was hard not to just share my faith stories with everyone I was staying with. However, the few weeks or so leading up to Arizona, I was in the thick of it. I was tired all the time, slightly burnt out, and I had not spent good quality time with God except on my driving days. It was getting hard, and I was only a little over a month into this four-month extravaganza. Traveling the country wasn't only getting harder—fulfilling my mission of sharing Jesus was. That was an issue.

Luckily, Shannon and I had FaceTimed quite a bit before I came to visit her, and we had grown comfortable with each other—as comfortable as you can be for meeting a stranger for multiple days in a state you aren't familiar with, that is. Since we'd been in contact for a while before we met, she knew the purpose of this trip and we had already talked beforehand about reading the Bible together.

On night one, it was time to read. I prayed beforehand that the Lord would speak to us through scripture, but when Shannon flipped open to a random page and we read it, to me, it meant nothing. However, to Shannon, it meant *everything*. She was ecstatic to tell me how she was encouraged and how the scripture spoke to her. That gave me encouragement. Let's go, God! (Keep in mind, without us predetermining we were going to read the Bible, the events to follow probably would not have happened.)

Earlier that night, Shannon told me that she was in an interesting place in her relationship with God. She expressed that she was a little confused about things and unsure about God, because she had been hurt by someone in the church before. But this Bible passage, she said, began to reopen a door to a relationship with him.

Remember, it is a *relationship* with God. People are imperfect. I am imperfect. The people within the church are imperfect. Some people who attend church will go to heaven, but some will also go to hell—I believe this. So please, remember that people are going to hurt you—in the church or outside of it.

People are going to falsely represent God because, once again, we are imperfect people. Thank goodness we have a *perfect savior*. If you are reading this and you have been hurt by "the church" or a person in the church, the good news is you were hurt by the person or the church, *not by God*. The good news is God will never hurt you and will only love you. Remember that.

My last night in Arizona, I was still lacking courage and boldness in my faith. When Shannon asked, that night, if we could pray together, *that was God*. That was God telling me to *be bold in my faith*. To pray for others and share him, even if it sometimes is a little awkward or uncomfortable. That was God reminding me the whole world is searching, but some just haven't found or heard yet. When God showed up for Shannon, that was God comforting me with the knowledge that when you are faltering and struggling, and you least expect it, he will show up for you. That when he wants to do something, he will do something. That was God reminding me that praying with someone else can bring hope, encouragement, and growth in faith to them *and* you.

That was *The Spark Plug*.

PRAY FOR HIS WILL

July 12 to July 16, 2021 - Oklahoma
Days 47 through 51

Tulsa, Oklahoma, was the first state I stayed in alone. About one-third of the way through the trip, I finally had some alone time. Four days, at that. I was so used to people having an itinerary for me that I didn't know what to do with myself—so, I gave it to God. I prayed to him and told him that I wanted him to guide this part of the trip and for his will to be done. I prayed specifically that if I was supposed to meet any people, he would put them in my path.

And that's what he did. Put people in my literal path.

I don't get lost often. Having a good sense of direction is something I take pride in. So when I got lost on my only hike in Oklahoma, I was quite humbled. I wish I could say I was frazzled due to the "beware of snakes" sign, and that's why I got lost. But that's not the truth—I simply just got lost on the long, winding path.

It was a short hike. I was only about one mile away from my car, so I knew I would find my way eventually. However, as the sun continued to set, finding my way back seemed more challenging by the second. But when I was lost and needed some direction, of course, *The Spark Plug* showed up.

Walking aimlessly, not seeing anyone for at least thirty minutes, I stumbled upon two people with their puppy. Like I said, normally I would appeal to my ego and tell myself "I got this," but not this time. I instantly interrupted their date night and asked if I could walk back with them to the parking lot.

Divine appointments are always so cool, because you never see them coming.

Ben and Kimber were happy to let me tag along the rest of the way. I was able to share the road trip and mention a huge part of my trip: God. Just like when Barb and I started to discuss our faith, something clicked between the couple and me. *When God is in the center, things just click.*

Ultimately, we arrived at the parking lot and I was extended an invite to their church the next evening.

Most of my trip, church services were attended over the radio in my gray 2010 Toyota Corolla. I wasn't going to miss an opportunity to attend in person. Admittedly, attending this church was a different experience for me, but it was a true blessing. To just take in a sermon with a welcoming community around was all I needed. And God knew it.

The rest of the Oklahoma stay, it was clear that God's will was for me to be "filled up," to rest and spend time with him and have my soul ignited for the rest of the trip. In the three other days, I was able to do many things I love. I slept, spoke on the phone intentionally with friends and family, was alone with God, and went rollerblading.

One other way that I love to be filled up is by playing volleyball. When I rollerbladed by multiple sand volleyball courts, I knew I needed to go. That evening, I drove to the courts and sat by, watching. That's when God taught me another valuable lesson: *his will is sometimes much easier to see if we take our steps.*

So many people, including myself, pray big prayers and have big expectations of God, then we sit and do nothing but wait. Is he capable of anything and everything? Yes. Is it always that simple? Heck no! God is a good father. Good parents want to teach their kids and give them the gifts and abilities to do amazing things, but they do not do everything for them.

After sitting alongside these sand volleyball courts for forty-five minutes, I realized no stranger was going to fly by and ask me to play with them. So, when I saw someone exit the court, I took the first step of courage by asking if I could join. That night, I played sand volleyball with strangers in Tulsa, Oklahoma, and it absolutely made my day.

I understand it's just volleyball, but it's something God put right in front of me, something that would fill me and give me life. All I had to do was *take the step* outward *in faith,* and then it was so easy to see his will.

Sometimes in life, you may find yourself completely lost. Or, you might know exactly where you want to go, with the answer right in front of you. God always knows the best direction. Seek him and trust his will. When he opens the door, take the step. Ask the couple to help guide you home, or ask the strangers to play volleyball. Simply ask God for his will to be done, and walk in the direction he guides. You won't be disappointed.

PRAY FOR MIRACLES

June 4 to June 8, 2021 - Utah
Days 9 through 13

One of Webster dictionary's kids definition's of the word miracle: an extraordinary event taken as a sign of the supernatural power of God. According to this definition, I have been blessed to see multiple miracles from God, both on my trip and in life.

Let me tell you about one of the miracles I saw in Utah—that's right, I experienced more than one miracle in Utah.

I was staying with Callie. You may have seen Callie on TikTok— she is known for making cricket noises in a huge lecture hall, causing her professor to comically try to find out where the bug is. It's quite an amazing gift actually—but enough about crickets.

Callie was super excited to take me around the whole state of Utah for adventures, and that's exactly what we did. We went to one state park and three national parks in four days: Goblin Valley, Arches National Park, Bryce Canyon National Park, and Zion National Park.

We had an amazing nighttime routine in our tent that consisted of reading the Bible, listening to Callie play "Fast Car" by Tracy Chapman on her guitar, and staring into the pitch black night sky full of millions of stars. The stars in Utah are indescribable.

During this part of the trip, it was confirmed to me that God is the God of Miracles, and also that when we really, truly depend on *The Spark Plug*, and I mean truly depend on him like he is all we need, he will show up. He will ignite the engine, because he *is* all we need.

After spending the day at Bryce Canyon and stopping at "Mossy Cave," we decided to find a camping spot. Callie had been driving her car all throughout Utah on our four-day adventure—I am talking hundreds of miles. Her sedan was similar in shape and size to my Toyota Corolla.

Callie had a perfect spot in mind to camp for the night. She had been there before—it was close to Zion National Park, the next day's adventure. It had been a full day already, and we pulled into the camp a couple hours short of dusk. There were not many spots available immediately, so we kept going. Callie pointed out that she saw a campsite on the right that she thought looked perfect.

Do you ever have a feeling in your gut that you're about to turn into trouble? When I saw how sandy this campsite was, I had that tingly feeling inside that things might not end well. Five seconds after our slow right turn into this beautiful campsite, we were stuck in a *terrible* campsite. The small car was stuck in the sand, and right away we knew that we were trapped.

With nightfall approaching, we needed to set up our tent sooner than later, but also did not want to be stuck in the sand the whole next day, as we had to drive hours back to Provo, Utah. The objective shifted from tent to car. It's quite comical to look back now, on what we did. We turned off the car, assigned ourselves to different tires, got on our hands and knees, and started digging. We had no tools but our hands. To paint a better picture, we were at least ninety feet from the road, and the sand had buried at least one-fifth of the tires. There was no way we were going to get out of this situation on our own.

After shoveling for about an hour with absolutely no ground made, Callie made the best point of the day—one I wish we had thought of sooner. Helpless, frustrated, and uncertain of how we would ever get out of this situation, she asked, "Should we pray?"

Of course we should pray! That's what we did. Callie led a prayer, asking God to help us out of this situation.

No one had driven by once in the hour we had been stuck, and it seemed completely hopeless. But sure enough, five minutes after praying, two men in a Jeep pulled up and asked if we needed any help. Another ten minutes later, we were free. An answered prayer. A miracle.

The coolest thing is: we *absolutely needed* God. On this trip, I needed God multiple times, and *every time* he showed up.

Back in my life of comfort, as I type this in my warm bed, I find it hard to "need" God as much. I work and make money. I spend my hard-earned money on my groceries and bills. I provide for myself. I fall into the trap of routine, half the time. I sometimes believe I am the one providing for myself, and without even trying, I forget how much I need God for every little thing in my life. I forget how he provides everything for me.

Let me remind you, whether you're stuck in life (or sand) or you feel like everything is figured out, you absolutely need God. Pray to him, tell him you need him daily, and I will not be surprised one bit if you see a miracle.

TO NOT PRAY

July 16 to July 19, 2021 - Arkansas
Days 51 through 54

> "Early the next morning Jesus went out to an isolated place" (Luke 4:42, NLT).

> "But Jesus often withdrew to the wilderness for prayer" (Luke 5:16, NLT).

> "Once Jesus was in a certain place praying" (Luke 11:1, NLT).

Multiple times in the Bible, it is clear that Jesus prayed. He was like the Michael Jordan of prayer. Dude was *just doing it*. He often went off on his own and spent time with his father. In all of the gospels, you can find multiple accounts of people looking for Jesus and finding that he was away in prayer in an isolated place. Not only did he pray, but he taught us how to pray and inspired us to do so:

> "But when you pray, go away by yourself, shut the door behind you, and pray to your father in private. Then your father, who sees everything, will reward you" (Matthew 6:6, NLT).

"If any of you wants to be my follower, you must give up your own way, take up your cross daily and follow me" (Luke 9:23, NLT).

Jesus set the precedent. He picked up his cross daily and spent intentional time with no one but his father.

On this trip, and still today, I easily forget the importance of spending intentional, prayerful time with God.

When I was in Arkansas with my friend, Hunter, who works in ministry, we went to church together. I had to fight against the urge to fall asleep the entire service. I was so tired and burned out at this point of the trip, and I couldn't figure out why—until I realized that while I went to multiple church services with Hunter, I still wasn't picking up my cross daily and being with my father, just me and him. I wasn't praying—meaning, I wasn't spending time with God.

Going to church like it's a checklist item isn't a relationship. Taking real time every day to place God as the priority *is*. So hear me when I say *The Spark Plug* needs to be *plugged in*. We need to be connected daily to him, intentionally. This trip taught me that not praying and not being in relationship with him can leave you empty, tired, and searching.

RECEIVING PRAYER

August 21 to August 23, 2021 - Delaware
Days 87 through 89

Jesus did spend time alone with his father, which was necessary. But he also spent time with his church. Although the church wasn't quite "the church" yet, he did have his ministry and his twelve disciples. Surely his disciples needed Jesus more than he needed them, but they were still imperative to his ministry. I am sure they encouraged him at times.

When I was in Delaware, the person I was staying with backed out one day before I arrived, and the girl I was currently smitten with ended "what could've been" over text message. Having been to church minimal times over the last three months of this trip, God's timing for a Sunday couldn't have been better. I woke up Sunday morning in Wilmington, Delaware and was able to attend Journey Church. Being in worship with others by my side and reflecting on how good he is brought me to tears.

Besides the elderly woman beside me who I had met at the beginning of the service, I knew no one, but I knew I needed prayer. When I saw the prayer team in the commons with no line, I slowly approached. Getting out of my comfort zone and asking this stranger for prayer was both filling and necessary. It was the encouragement I needed to remind myself that this was God's trip, not mine. God's plan, not mine.

During this trip, so many times, I needed to be alone with God, but I also needed encouragement from other believers. I needed their prayer and their fellowship.

Receiving prayer in Delaware taught me this relationship with God is meant to be with him, but also with others. To be one-on-one *and* communal. To grow your personal relationship with him and to grow his Kingdom.

PRAY FOR OPPORTUNITIES

Shawn Johnson, the Red Rocks Pastor, once delivered a sermon about how he had prayed for opportunities to share Jesus, and sure enough, he had multiple opportunities shortly afterward. Ever since, I've done the same. It is amazing how God answers prayers.

I have had conversations about Jesus everywhere from bars to the audition line for CBS's *Survivor*.

On the trip, when I felt burned out, insecure, or lacking in faith, I prayed not just for opportunities, but for boldness and strength to actually share Jesus and my story.

Multiple times, I felt uncertain of how much fire I had in me to get out of my comfort zone and share him. I was afraid of forcing it and doing it unnaturally. You know, it's actually not a comfortable thing to meet strangers across the entire United States, but every time I felt that way, God opened up a door and answered the prayer.

Boston, New Jersey, Tennessee, and Michigan—God gave me multiple opportunities to share him, and these were always amazing, fruitful, and filling conversations with people who had all different types of beliefs, from different walks of life. God knows exactly what he is doing. Pray for opportunities. He will give you the courage and the words.

PRAY BIG PRAYERS

Big prayers are scary, because…what if they happen? Really, they are scarier to the enemy, because bigger prayers show proof of a bigger God. My prayer for this book is that it impacts one million people, however that looks to God. If only one person reads this book, even if it's just me, and they go on to share Jesus with someone else, setting off a chain reaction of Jesus, that would be the *biggest win ever*.

Here is my prayer: Father, God, thank you so much for this amazing life. Thank you for every blessing. When we fall so short, you are there to pick us up. Thank you so much for this relationship we are blessed to be able to have with you. God, I pray that through this book—your book—you impact one million people. I don't care how it looks. If only one person reads this, that's okay. I want souls to be impacted because of this book—not sales, souls. Father, this life is yours and this book is yours. I pray whoever is reading this, wherever they are, that you impact their soul with your love. Thank you for being such an amazing God. Amen.

Pray for anything. Pray for everything.

Don't worry about anything; instead pray about everything. Tell God what you need, and thank him for all he has done. Then you will experience God's peace, which exceeds anything we can understand. His peace will guard your hearts and your minds as you live in Christ Jesus. (Phil. 4:6-7, NLT)

He doesn't say he will answer every prayer, but that we will experience his peace. He gives us something much better than every answered prayer—he gives us the ability to have a real relationship with him, the ability to trust and rely on him, and the ability to experience a little slice of heaven, *his peace*, on this earth. That's what prayer is. Not asking him for everything, but being able to *be with him through everything.*

Nike has been "just doing it" since 1964. He has been doing it since forever. Pray. Just pray.

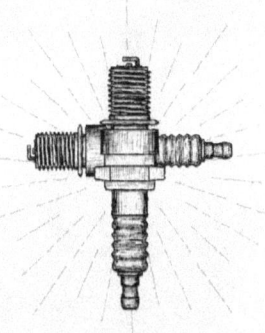

Do not Worry

June 11 to June 25, 2021 - Montana, Wyoming, Washington, Oregon
Days 16 through 30

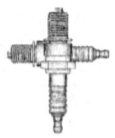

I worry a lot—about the future, about the past, about everything. I worry way too much.

I once heard a sermon about the fact that we often think so much about our past and our future that we barely have time to focus on the here and now. This is what Jesus says about worrying about tomorrow:

> That is why I tell you not to worry about everyday life—whether you have enough food and drink, or enough clothes to wear. Isn't life more than food, and your body more than clothing? Look at the birds. They don't plant or harvest or store food in barns, for your heavenly Father feeds them. And aren't you far more valuable to him than they are? Can all your worries add a single moment to your life?
>
> And why worry about your clothing? Look at the lilies of the field and how they grow. They don't work or make their clothing, yet Solomon in all his glory was not dressed as beautifully as they are. And if God cares so wonderfully for wildflowers that are here today and thrown into the fire tomorrow, he will certainly care for you. Why do you have so little faith?

So don't worry about these things, saying, 'What will we eat? What will we drink? What will we wear?' These things dominate the thoughts of unbelievers, but your heavenly Father already knows all your needs. Seek the Kingdom of God above all else, and live righteously, and he will give you everything you need.

So don't worry about tomorrow, for tomorrow will bring its own worries. Today's trouble is enough for today. (Matthew 6:25-34, NLT)

This scripture from the Sermon on the Mount is so easy to hear and be encouraged by. It is so hard to believe, accept, and let it change your life. Truthfully, I am still working on the belief, acceptance, and life alteration Jesus talks about here. My whole life was turned upside down this last year, and it has been extremely challenging to not worry about "what's next" or "the next big thing". But God has shown me glimpses of what it looks like to not worry and to fully trust him. That is what I am aspiring to do. Every. Single. Day.

Montana is where God told me to stop worrying about anything and start trusting him in everything.

Izzi was one of the original people I had spoken with about hosting me; she committed to being my host in Bozeman, Montana. Our relationship was special from the beginning, since we were both at a place of excitement and newness in our relationship with God. I think that is why we had such a great connection and bonded instantly, because the foundation was Jesus.

Izzi and I FaceTimed often and became great friends well before my trip to Montana. Such great friends, in fact, that on the fourth day of us hanging out together, we got into a fight. I was blessed to be able to fight with Izzi in the third week of my road trip. Why was that a blessing? Because it was proof that I was comfortable enough to let my guard down.

It can be easier to fight with someone you love rather than a stranger, and that's exactly what this situation was. It felt like a fight with my best friend whom I had known for years. The point is, God's timing is always impeccable. I was weeks into my trip and had been "on my toes" or "on my best behavior" for much of that time. God blessed me with Izzi so I could truly take a deep breath, relax, be my true self, and enjoy things…for the most part.

There was something in the back of my mind that was not letting me fully breathe, relax, and enjoy my time with Izzi: the paralyzing attribute I call "worry." My worry stemmed from something that I still worry about to this day: the future. What's next? Where is God taking me? Who is God going to bring into my life? What should I do next?

These questions can be okay to help us find a plan and choose a direction, but when you let them overtake your every thought, they turn into worry, overthinking, and anxiety. We begin trying to control things rather than trusting God is in control, and this is a major problem.

After Montana, I was fully prepared to spend four days in Washington, followed by four days in Oregon. Exciting! Well, it would have been, if I knew who I was staying with, where I would be staying, or what I would be doing.

My comrades from Washington and Oregon had either ghosted me or messaged me only days in advance to tell me they were going to be out of the state at that time. I don't know about you, but when planning a cross-country road trip for nine months, I prefer the plans to be concrete before I am already in the middle of the trip! Backing out at the last minute after nine months of commitment was like telling me that they didn't want to parent with me a week before our baby was born!

Anyway, my plans were not going as planned—who would've thought? As I should have learned from the Shake-A-Day or my stay with Barb, even when plans don't work out, God's got this—but sometimes, I can be stubborn.

Instead of trusting God and relaxing in Montana like he had planned for me, I decided to worry about what was to come. Despite my worry, the first three days, we did some amazing things in Bozeman. On Night One, Izzi was ecstatic to show me one of the most extravagant sunset views I have ever seen. We drove a few miles out of town, blasted "Jireh" by Elevation Worship and Maverick City Music, and ended up in front of a beautiful mountain. Izzi and her gorgeous blonde puppy, Florence, showed me one of their favorite spots. Izzi played the guitar and sang original songs for me as I watched from a huge rock I had climbed.

On Day Two, Saturday, we hiked Hyalite Trail and ended up at Palisade Falls. Palisade Falls had a waterfall streaming down a giant cliff. I stuck my medium-long, dirty hair into the waterfall and had one of those special moments I will never forget as the crystal ice water flowed over my head.

Afterward, we sat by a stream and had deep conversation for hours. We then went back to town and enjoyed Bozeman Beach with Izzi's brother, Sam. To cap off the evening, we read the Bible. Unsure of what to read, I threw my Bible onto the bed and it opened right to Mathew 6:25-34. Knowing this scripture by heart, instead of reading this scripture about not worrying—which I desperately needed to hear—I suggested to Izzi we find something else to read. I can be dumb, sometimes.

Day Three—there's something about the number three. The holy trinity, the father, the son, and the holy spirit. The number of days before Jesus rose from the grave. The number I rolled playing the Shake-A-Day...and the number of times God spoke to me in Montana before I finally listened.

Day Three was jam packed. Florence graduated from puppy preschool, Izzi brought me to her church, we went to a river nearby to baptize one of Izzi's friends and see him give his life to Christ, we traveled to Yellowstone National Park, and we capped off the night with s'mores.

From hearing all that day entailed, I am sure you would say it sounds like a great day, but it was not just a great day—it was a life-changing day.

Let me remind you—during these three days, I was worried the whole time. I had amazing experiences, but I was not fully present in any of them. My mind was always wondering what I would be doing the next week when I headed to Washington. I could have truly enjoyed the amazing things listed above if I fully surrendered my worry to God and trusted in his provision, if I believed the scripture that says, "Do not worry about tomorrow," and, "Seek the Kingdom of God above all else, and live righteously, and he will give you everything you need."

Although I was being stubborn and holding onto control, he didn't let that stop him. Even when we are stubborn, lacking faith, and being a little silly, *The Spark Plug* still shows up.

Remember, on Day One, how we sang "Jireh" in the car? (*Pause.* I have to add this because literally this second the song Jireh just came on through my earbuds from Pandora. God is so good. That is the spark plug who provides and loves us so much. Wow. God is good.)

What I did not mention is how "Jireh" ends. It refers to scripture: "If he dresses the lilies with beauty and splendor, how much more will he clothe you? If he watches over every sparrow, how much more will he love you?" (Matthew 6:25-34, NLT).

You might be piecing this together on your own—on Day Two, my Bible had landed wide open, specifically on the scripture Matthew 6:25-34.

Well, if that's not enough for you, this should be: you will never guess what Sunday morning's sermon at Izzi's church was on. The *whole* sermon was specifically on the scripture in Matthew 6:25-34.

Bam. It finally clicked; I finally put the pieces together. God spoke to me three days in a row through song, scripture, and sermon. I finally heard him. The simplest message ever from our father: *do not worry.*

After church, I could not wait to tell Izzi all about my revelation and what God had spoken to me. We were both so excited and thrilled that God told me not to worry—but then I got to thinking, "He doesn't want me to worry, but how in the world do I not worry when next week I am supposed to stay in a part of the country I have never been to before with no plans?"

Trusting God is hard. But so worth it.

There was an increase in my belief that God was going to do something. I was now not worried, but rather really curious and eager to figure out what he was going to do.

That Sunday evening, when Izzi and I rolled into Yellowstone to meet my cousin and her fiancé for a couple nights, I was surprised to see two other people there.

See, I had planned for months to stay with my cousin, Morgan, and her fiancé, Tayt, when I visited this part of the country. I knew that part of the plan—I just didn't know the whole plan. It turned out there were also two girls who were staying with them on this leg of the trip. It also turned out that I just happened to know one of these girls, Karissa, from college back home. It *also* just so happened that Karissa and the other girl, Kaykay were both headed to Washington and Oregon the following week.

And it just so happened that I was able to join them.

That was that. I was in awe of God. He spoke to me loud and clear and told me, "Stephen, do not worry."

The next week of the trip worked out so perfectly. Izzi and I went off on our own to explore the Grand Tetons and Jackson Hole, Wyoming. We accidentally hiked eleven miles at Jenny Lake, thinking it was going to be five miles. We cliff jumped, as many strangers stood either in awe of our bravery or dumbfounded by our stupidity. We saw a grizzly bear, way closer than I like to remember.

Back at Bozeman, we summited Mount Sacajawea. We floated down the Madison River as I was blessed to share my testimony for the seventh time of the trip. We dressed up for a fancy dinner, tipping a waiter hundreds of dollars that were donated to me for the trip. And we went back to Izzi's sunset spot and danced on top of her car with worship music blasting. That was how my Montana trip ended.

Washington and Oregon were just as amazing. God blessed me with my first night alone at a hotel in Spokane. He blessed me with some of the most beautiful experiences of my life with Karissa and KayKay, such as hiking to Colchuck Lake in Leavenworth, WA and Blue Pool in Oregon. Both of those hikes ended with me submerged in the coldest and most beautiful water I had ever experienced in my life. We slept in a tent every night and spent time in a different park every day. This was absolutely the most lovely portion of the whole trip.

The last day of Oregon was the biggest blessing of all, when I parted from the girls and found a campsite on my own. I set up camp, built a fire, and slept in a tent. That night by the fire was one of the most peaceful moments I've ever had. I was able to reflect on the last week or so. I was able to sit in gratitude, awe, and wonder of our amazing God. That last week was awesome not only because of the experiences I had with others, but because I chose to finally surrender my worries to God. I chose to trust him and let him worry for me. And he absolutely provided.

From paralyzing worry to breathtaking amazement—that is what our God does. He tells you that your plans are changing, but urges you to trust in him because he knows what he is doing. He changes your plans for so many reasons—to avoid getting hurt, because someone else needs you, to grow your faith, or maybe to bring you to one of the most beautiful sights and experiences of your life.

Worrying will not add a moment to your life. He cares for you so much more than the birds, whom he also faithfully provides for. You are so valuable to him, so seek his Kingdom above all else with righteousness, and he will give you everything you need. Do not worry. Do not worry. Do not worry.

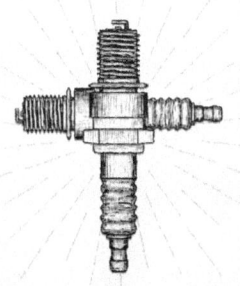

JEHOVAH JIREH

ehovah Jireh: God will provide.

As the song "Jireh" and the scripture Matthew 6:25-34 point out, God is a God who provides.

"Seek the Kingdom of God above all else, and live with righteousness, and he will give you everything you need" (Matthew 6:33, NLT).

Note: it does not state he will give you everything you desire and more—only *everything you need*. But what is a need? In this season of my life, it is really easy to sit here and say I need: a girlfriend, a career I am confident in, more money—the list is endless. Sadly, the truth is, I do not need any of those things. Everything that I need, God has provided.

The most comforting feeling is knowing God knows better than I do. He knows what blessings I can handle. He knows what blessings I cannot handle.

Hard truth: I am still growing and learning, and honestly I am not quite ready to lead a woman in a Godly relationship. God recognizes I'm not quite ready, even when I don't. If I had a full-time career at this point in my life, plus a girlfriend, I would absolutely not have time to write this book—something I believe God wants me to do. I make enough money right now to pay the bills I have, so other than security, I really don't need more money right now. God is never ahead and he is never behind. He provides, and he does so right on time.

This whole trip, God provided right. On. Time.

God provided so much, but in just a few ways, God provided through a friend at a vineyard, through time with my mom, and through finances.

WINE COUNTRY

June 27 to June 30, 2021 - California
Days 32 through 35

The Spark Plug always wins—we've covered that. However, that doesn't negate the fact that there is an enemy who is always trying to steal, kill, and destroy. When I made my first stop in California, I was ecstatic to be in Fresno with Hanna and her family. They lived on their own vineyard and had a guest house just for me.

During this trip, I had slept in a tent on God's bumpy, crafted floor without showering for at least fourteen days. I've slept in an RV, on a hairy couch with multiple dogs, in sketchy motel beds, and more. Having a guest house to myself in Fresno easily takes the cake.

The first night was amazing. They didn't just own a winery, but they hosted parties there. I arrived right on time to enjoy a "white party"—a fancy gathering where everyone dresses in all white. It reminded me of a high school football game "white out" theme, just way more elegant. We celebrated. We tasted delicious wine slushies and rocked the back patio dance floor under the California sunset. The remainder of my time in Fresno had many joyful moments, too, like floating down miles of a river that was literally in their backyard, hugging mammoth trees at Sequoia National Park, and canoeing with Hanna and her future fiancé, Sawyer, at Hume Lake. Joy was the overall highlight of this portion of the trip—but the enemy tried to steal it all on the second day.

Gabrielle was Hanna's good friend who worked at the winery as a server. Her heart was beautiful. She was so kind and welcoming. She was going to be a missionary overseas, and she had the light of Jesus in her. After spinning her around on the dance floor the first night we met, I definitely had a crush on her.

As mentioned, God is still preparing me for my wife today, so I was most definitely not ready for her when I was twenty-five. I thought I was ready. I thought Gabrielle could be her. I thought instantly that God had put her in my path for a reason. Well, read on if you want to see what happens when you idolize something and let your brain set super high, unrealistic expectations of that "idol."

The morning after dancing like I never had before, I was more than ready to serenade Gabrielle on the river float. At one point, she had fallen behind quite a ways and—being the intentional man I am—I dragged my feet a little harder to slow down. I was excited to get to know her better and tell her all about myself. She asked, "What's your story?" This was the moment. Hook. Line. Sinker… or so I thought.

I think this shows very clearly that I was not ready for my wife. I thought my testimony could be used as a sort of pick-up line—as if my testimony is about anything but God. He gets all the credit, and I partially forgot that. Regardless, just as I was starting the story of how God worked in my life, Gabrielle got distracted and someone else on a tube entered the picture. All of a sudden, she was in conversation with someone else and we weren't even talking anymore.

To Gab's, she probably just assumed this conversation would continue later, when we weren't floating down a river with ten other people. To the devil, he saw a wide open door, a chance to steal, kill, and destroy. An opportunity to tell me the lies: "She doesn't want to hear your story," "She would never like you," "You are not a real man of God." It can happen that fast, if you aren't careful. From crushing on Gabrielle to being crushed by Gabrielle (really, by the enemy), it was a 180-degree turn. I felt the flip, and I wore the flip on my sleeve. I completely shut down.

After having a hard time "being me" or feeling "comfortable in my own skin" for the next couple hours, I found myself sitting in Hanna's backyard. I had a grilled weenie, a burned marshmallow, and a beautiful sunset in the background, but I was still crushed. You should never be crushed when eating a grilled weenie!

That's when God provided Hanna and taught me that sometimes, you're just one conversation, prayer, or second away from breakthrough. Hanna, being the bubbly, kind-hearted person she was, engaged in an intentional conversation with me. Within minutes of being open and vulnerable with Hanna, we easily diagnosed this as a case of overthinking and the enemy giving it his best college try. After that quick talk, I was back. I was up and playing catch with Hannah, Gabrielle, Sawyer, and Hanna's brothers. I was back with a smile and joy.

The first thing in Genesis, the first book in the Bible, that God says is "not good" is for man to be alone.

"Then the Lord God said, "It is not good for the man to be alone" (Genesis 18a, NLT).

The enemy wants you isolated. He wants you to avoid community. He wants you to shy away from God and others and hold all the weight of your thoughts and feelings inside. *Don't do it. Don't let him win.* And even if you sit in it for a while, remember:

God will provide. He will provide a way out. He will provide a Hanna. So when he does provide a way out, hop on that train as fast as you can and don't look back. *The Spark Plug* is moving and wants you to hang on for the joyful ride.

SHERI

July 19 to July 28 - Texas, Louisiana, Mississippi
Days 54 through 63

My mom, Sheri, is an amazing woman. Let me tell you why: Sheri loves. She loves gracefully, fearlessly, and past the point that most people would love others—when they probably don't deserve it anymore. She loves God, she loves her children, and she loves anyone that she comes into contact with, especially the people who are sometimes difficult to love (this can be me). God places people in her life who desperately need love, and she shows them the love of Jesus, every day. In many ways, Sheri emulates the love of Jesus.

God provided me time with my mom on this trip to remind me of what life with Jesus is like: freeing, scary, unpredictable, joyous, exciting, and full of grace, authenticity, and never-ending love.

Sheri's first act of love and selflessness was taking eight days off of her full time job to meet me in the middle of the country. Eight days! That included eight days of hotels, food, and travel expenses—eight days of paying for herself and her son.

Arkansas was a hard stay for me—I was tired, burned out, and not properly leaning on my relationship with the Lord. The timing couldn't have been better to pick up my mom from the Little Rock airport. Like with Izzi, I felt finally able to breathe now that I was with my mom, someone who knows me better than anyone in the world.

One of the first moments I remember with my mom was one of joy and laughter. Driving to Dallas, we stopped at the Texarkana exit to indulge in some Whataburger, some of the best fast food burgers in the country (I am aware this is up for debate). On the way out of town, Sheri did a mom thing and said we should stop at the local grocery store. I was focused on getting to Dallas, but moms do know best. We stopped in the local grocery store. It wasn't crowded. My mom went to a stand of flip flops and wanted to try on a pair. She said they were an extremely good deal at three dollars per pair—then, two seconds later, one of the flip flops tore straight in half, before she even had the chance to try it on. This is one of the few moments of my life I have seen her laugh hysterically, which led me to being unable to hold back my own giggles and snorts. With that preview of what the rest of the grocery store would look like, we opted to leave and continue on our path down south.

The rest of our long drive down to Dallas included singing our lungs out to old country songs, including one of our favorites, "Austin" by Blake Shelton. I was embracing my southern look, wearing my cowboy hat (named "Remi") that I purchased in Montana. It was a night of joy and comfort, things that are always offered in the presence of *The Spark Plug*.

The next morning, we woke up in Dallas, TX. At my height of 6'2", my head was practically bursting through our hotel ceiling, so we figured it would be best to get outside. Mom unpacked her rollerblades, and it was go time.

Side story: I first realized how rollerblades are a lot like Jesus a couple years ago, when I saw an extremely cute girl rollerblading down our local trail back home. She was blonde and wore Ray-Bans with a neon winter hat—she looked like she should live in Colorado. I instantly got to thinking that I needed a pair of rollerblades, for a couple reasons: 1) I loved rollerblading when I was a kid, and

I remember it brought me great joy, peace, freedom, and many more feelings, and 2) a really cute girl was rollerblading. Maybe, if I bought a pair and went on the trail, I would see her again.

I saw something that she had and I knew that I wanted it. I wanted to be a part of it, from just that little taste of it. After I bought my own pair and took them out, I forgot all about the girl—but I did remember the joy, love, freedom, and peace that rollerblading brought to my life. I had to tell someone—no. *I had to tell everyone.*

I told my roommate, Grayden, my good friend, Joelle, and of course my mom, Sheri. Within the next month, we all had rollerblades, and I was fortunate enough to share this amazing experience with each of them. I don't know if the chain reaction of rollerblading stopped there or continued, but here is what I do know: rollerblading is like Jesus. Once you experience him in your heart and what he truly has to offer you—life transformation, peace, love, joy, freedom, and so much more—you can't help but tell others about him. Once you tell others about him, you want them to experience him too, and to experience him together in community. So yeah, Jesus is kinda the rollerblade king. How gnarly!

Back to the mom story. We decided to rollerblade on a trail in Dallas that would give us a beautiful view of the city skyline. The only problem: the beginning of the trail had the steepest decline I had seen in my life, from a rollerblading perspective. Mom, making the smart call, began to unstrap and decided she would walk down the hill. Not me. You see, even at twenty-five, I don't think the male brain is fully developed. There's a reason we die earlier than women. I stared down the mountain ahead and started reciting scripture in my head.

"Be strong and courageous! Do not be afraid or discouraged. For the Lord your God is with you wherever you go" (Joshua 1:9, NLT).

I know this is completely out of context and I don't think scripture should be used that way, but if it is done to help you trust the Lord to get you down a giant hill on tiny wheels, I think it's more than okay. I'd rather put God and his word into everything I do rather than just some things I do.

Just like *Mario Kart, three…two…one…go!* I was off. Instant regret. I was so scared, but you know what else? *I was so free.* They say when we are facing the most excitement in life, we feel the most free. I went down that hill quicker than an Olympian skier. I managed to stay on my feet, and even coasted for a solid forty-five seconds once I hit flat ground.

God reminded me that day that hills are scary, solo road trips are scary, and life is really scary, but when we face that fear head on with Jesus in our hearts, he will provide freedom.

You know what else can be scary? Meeting a stranger you FaceTimed for the first time the day before…with your mom. But we did it. That night, we met Ellen, who took us to "Son of a Butcher" for some fire barbecue, followed by a sermon at The Porch Church. Arriving at The Porch, I wasn't sure if we'd arrived at a church or a concert. With the amount of people I saw came confidence that I do have a future wife out there. If they can fit that many God-fearing women inside of one building, then God can fit one woman into my life, right? Regardless, Mom and I faced the fear of meeting someone new together, and then we experienced a night of worship and praise to Jesus.

Next, God provided excitement. Mom was set on taking me to a restaurant called The Oasis the next night in Austin, TX, which had a beautiful overlook of Lake Travis. Although there was a light drizzle, Mom and I opted to wait an extra thirty minutes to have outside seats on the patio—and I am so glad we did. This meal stands out in my memory not because of the really great meal with

Mom—actually, the real excitement was provided when Mom was not present at the table. It came from Ashlyn, who was our server. She had long brunette hair that caught my eye the second we sat down. I love these moments—I become slightly nervous, as my heart starts to beat a little faster, becoming completely distracted. Sorry, Mom. I was distracted most of the meal.

When Sheri got up to use the restroom, I knew I had a small window of time. There is something super embarrassing about introducing yourself to a girl in front of your mom, so I had to do it now, while she was gone. I took my shot when Ashlyn came back—I got her number and Instagram! And…honestly, nothing really came from it. But one thing did: after starting to become burned out in Arkansas, God gave me adrenaline, excitement, and newfound life for my adventure with the *The Spark Plug*.

Grace, authenticity, and never-ending love is what life with Jesus looks like. It's also what life with Sheri looks like. Remember how I said that it's easier to fight with the ones you love? Yeah…it is easiest to fight with my mom. And this week had its moments. Whether stopping the car on an onramp headed to the interstate, going at each other while driving through a torrential downpour, or walking away from each other in the middle of Bourbon Street in New Orleans, we had our moments.

I think God provided something really special here, though. Every single time we fought, we apologized and were able to reconnect even deeper. One fight led to me sharing my full testimony, which I had never told her in full. Another led to a really great conversation, full of vulnerability, over a glass of wine. They all led to a deeper level of understanding of each other and how we function. Although I wouldn't recommend it consistently, fighting can actually be healthy.

Don't miss what is so special about this. Every time I talk to my mom about this trip or any other adventures, she always refers back to the amazing memories we made together.

She talks about the beautiful sunrise at a secret spot in Austin, all the goofy moments of booking a bunch of different hotels and canceling reservations in hopes of getting a pool, taking a three-hundred picture photoshoot of me in Galveston along the beach, throwing pizza crust into the air to feed hundreds of seagulls outside our hotel window, going on a log ride with children who seemed to have parents nowhere near, seeing huge snakes on Bourbon Street, gambling in our hotel in Biloxi, MS, or just resting and watching *The Office*. The list is endless, and she only remembers all the good times. She remembers how much she loves her son, no matter what condition he is in.

I remember things a little differently. I remember being short tempered, impatient, or getting into a fight with her for absolutely no reason. I hold these feelings still, and although my mom accepted my apologies multiple times, I still have a hard time accepting her grace, mercy, and never-ending love. I have a hard time accepting that I am forgiven, and forgiving myself.

My mom remembers driving back to our hotel in the dark night, watching me sing, "See a Victory" with the sunroof open and windows down. Meanwhile, I forget her love for me and accept the shame around my behaviors, shame that isn't coming from her.

This part of the trip reminded me of the most important thing of all: the gospel of Jesus Christ.

> Can anything ever separate us from Christ's love? Does it mean he no longer loves us if we have trouble or calamity, or are persecuted, or hungry, or destitute, or in danger, or threatened with death?

No, despite all these things, overwhelming victory is ours through Christ, who loved us.

And I am convinced that nothing can ever separate us from God's love. Neither death nor life, neither angels nor demons, neither our fears today nor our worries about tomorrow– not even the powers of hell can separate us from God's love. No power in the sky above or in earth below—indeed, nothing in all creation will ever be able to separate us from God that is revealed in Jesus our Lord. (Romans 8:35-39, NLT)

Jesus made the ultimate sacrifice for us. But he didn't do it so we could live shameful lives; he did it so we could experience true freedom, both now on this earth and forever in eternity. He forgave me even before I was a sinner.

Likewise, my mom forgave me before I was ever a "bad" son. And that's not even what she sees—she sees an amazing son who has bad moments, and she forgets those moments the second they happen because she loves him that much.

The Spark Plug already forgave you. He loves you so much. His grace and mercy is ever flowing, and the relationship with him is real and authentic. All you have to do is accept him.

And that's why God provided me time with Sheri. To remind me of Jesus.

MONEY, MONEY, MONEY, MONEY...MONEY

"I know all the things you do, and I have opened a door for you that no one can close" (Revelation 3:8a, NLT).

Nothing can close a door that God has opened, and no one can open a door that God has closed. God opened the door to this trip and he was not closing it. In order to ensure this trip was seen all the way through, God provided.

Sheri did another amazing thing for me on this trip that God absolutely was involved in. I love how God works so much through other people in our lives.

I have always been the creative type. I like to think outside of the box. For example, I have a highly developed gift system for my niece and nephews every Christmas. Their first Christmas, they get one penny, one letter with a life lesson, and one gift. Each year, as they grow, so does the gift. Every year, the money doubles until they are eighteen years old, always attached with a new life lesson and gift. After they graduate, I may not ever be able to get them another gift again, or else I'll be broke—but I'm committed to the system. I guess It's a good thing God provides, even financially.

I love to mix my creativity with grandiose gestures. Sheri, knowing me, decided to return the favor and give me such a gift for the trip. She gave me three large bags. What was in these bags was exactly what I needed at so many points of the trip: envelopes. There were all sorts of envelopes—different shapes, sizes, and colors. Each envelope had a date on it, the date it was to be opened. I did not count, but there had to have been at least 100 envelopes.

As the trip unfolded, I began to open these letters and realize the true gift they really were. There were letters from family members, friends, my mom's friends, members from her Bible study whom I never met, customers from the bar I had worked at, and so on. I was so shocked by some of the letters I received and who they were from.

God worked through these letters. Some were funny when I needed a laugh. Some were heartfelt when I needed love. Some were encouraging when I was thinking of quitting. They were all opened in perfect timing. God knew exactly what date I was supposed to read these letters when he asked them, through my mom, to put a "random" date on their envelopes.

God provided so much encouragement through these letters, but he also provided in another way: financially. It can be easy to worry about money, but what did we talk about at the beginning of this chapter? Seek him righteously and he will give you everything you need. So when I opened up a letter from my mom's friend, Mike, and it had hundreds of dollars in it, I was shocked. When I was in Nashville and received a letter from my uncle that had a cross and seven hundred dollars, I was in awe.

Aside from the letters, God provided so much through others. The day I left, Jon from my Bible study slipped me a 100 dollar bill. Barb made sure in Colorado I paid for absolutely no food. After leaving Callie in Utah, thirty minutes onto the interstate, I realized my wipers held a tiny card tucked under them, which held a fifty dollar bill. Being bored on some drives, I reopened my investment account and made thousands of dollars in the stock market from a few simple trades.

Now, here is the jaw dropper: on August 5, 2021, exactly twenty-four states through my forty-eight state road trip, I had spent $5,484.22. In seventy-two days, traveling across exactly half of the country, I had only spent a little over five thousand dollars. Not bad at all—but there's more. Seventy-two days through this trip, through investments or donations, with no income, I had made $5,054.02. Yes, I am telling you that I spent seventy-two days traveling half of the country, and only lost $430.42. A door that God has flung open cannot be closed.

I was fully expecting to use all of the money I had to my name on this trip, yet when I got home, I still had money to pay the bills, buy groceries, and provide for myself for months until I found my next job. But the truth is, *I* didn't provide any of it. God did. God did it all.

Emotionally, spiritually, financially—any and every way possible—God will provide. He is Jehovah Jireh. He is the God who provides.

No matter where you are in life right now, what you are faced with, what you have (or don't have), trust him. He knows best, better than our stubborn selves. He is never late, and he is never early—he is always right on time.

Seek the Kingdom of God above all else and with righteousness, and he will give you everything you need.

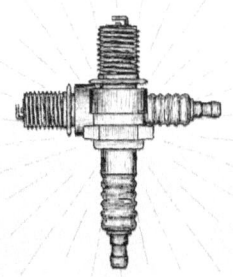

DO NOT BE AFRAID

June 4 to June 8, 2021 - Utah
Days 9 through 13
July 9 to July 12 - New Mexico
Days 44 through 47
June 11 to June 19, 2021 - Montana, Wyoming
Days 16 through 24

*C*allie and I were having a blast on our hike through Bryce Canyon National Park—exploring God's creation and just taking it in. The energy I get when I am exploring God's beauty is hard to match—it's that fun, goofy, excitable energy that makes me want to just randomly do push ups in the middle of a hike—so that's what I did.

After knocking out my ten push ups, I shot up and stood in awe of God's creation. The little squirrel that was no more than ten feet away from me seemed to be doing the same thing, while overlooking a cliff.

Then—*strike!* It had been blending in with the desert floor, but suddenly, a long, scaly, and—might I add—creepy rattlesnake struck at its prey.

I am *deathly* afraid of snakes. Not just rattlesnakes—any snake of any shape, size, or color. They produce a fear in me that is hard to explain. Whenever I see a snake, my whole body typically shudders. Then, nine times out of ten, I flee faster than Usain Bolt. I am gone. It is so reactionary and I lose so much control, that I could be with the most beautiful woman on the earth, or the most prominent president in the world—heck, I could be with Jesus himself, and I would still dash away. That is the kind of fear snakes instill in me.

But in this situation, I didn't run. It was the one-out-of-ten scenario. I held my ground. I didn't flee, but I sure as heck didn't fight. I stood still. Fear, awe, and multiple other sensations went through my body as my friend Callie laughed, recording the ghostly look on my face. I faced fear head on, then slowly inched away, while warning other hikers coming.

I believe this is what Jesus expects of us, plus more. I believe that he desires for us to be fearless—and this isn't just a hunch. This is biblical. In the Bible, it says "do not be afraid" 365 times, one for each day of the year. God wants us to not just be afraid, but to be fearless, every single day.

Now, there is healthy fear, which protects us. If I didn't have a rational fear of this rattlesnake, maybe I would have fearlessly gone and picked it up, slinging it around my neck like a toy. There is a difference between being fearless and being stupid. I have to remind myself of this often.

Most of the time, though, we allow unhealthy fear into our lives and live in it. Unhealthy fear isn't for protection; it debilitates and destroys. Unhealthy fear will keep us from facing the things we fear and limit what God can do in our lives, if we let it.

New Mexico with Kate was awesome, but I admit, I definitely was a chicken at times. *But*, I was a chicken that grew wings and could fly. I crossed the road and lived to tell the story. I didn't remain wingless or stay on the "safe side."

Story number one: The Airbnb was a log cabin in the middle of nowhere. We were surrounded by thousands of giant trees. Everything about it was perfect, especially the pitch black night sky, which allowed us to see millions of stars. However, when it was time for bed, the black sky made me feel a little uneasy. Especially the first night, when we were both lying down on opposite sides of the room, and the motion light right outside our front door went off. There was that feeling again—instant, paralyzing fear.

"Hey Kate," I whispered, "Did you see that? Are you awake? Kate? Kate. Kate!"

She was awake. She also wasn't half as afraid as I was. Until five minutes later, when the motion light went off again. And again. And again. Luckily, I had Kate to help subdue some of this fear. We talked through it, until we inevitably slept.

Sure enough, it happened the next night, too.

Kate and I never did find out who or what was outside setting off our motion light, but we did learn something from it: we don't always have to face fear alone. God gives us each other so we can walk side by side through fear. He also gives us something else pretty important: himself. God gives us the Holy Spirit and the armor of God.

The fruits of the Spirit, found in Galatians 5:22, include love, joy, peace, patience, kindness, goodness, faithfulness, gentleness, and self-control. None of these sound like fear.

The armor of God includes the belt of truth, the body armor of God's righteousness, the shoes of peace, the shield of faith, salvation as your helmet, and the sword of spirit. The Bible specifically says to "put on every piece of God's armor so you will be able to resist the enemy in the time of evil" (Ephesians 6:13, NLT).

God tells us to not be afraid every. Single. Day. He sure isn't the one producing the fear—the enemy is. "Be strong in the Lord and in his mighty power. Put on all of God's armor so that you will be able to stand firm against all strategies of the devil. For we are not fighting against flesh-and-blood enemies" (Ephesians 6:10-12a, NLT).

We don't have to be afraid, but when fear does arise, we have God. We have the Holy Spirit. We have his protection and truth, and we have those whom he blesses us with to get through those moments. We have *The Spark Plug*. Do not be afraid.

Story number two: another snake story. While gleefully skipping down the mountain Kate and I had just hiked for hours, minutes away from the car, we faced a road block. This snake wasn't nearly as large as the rattlesnake in Utah, but nonetheless, it was a snake. And it was in our way.

I had a few options. 1) Wait the snake out from a safe distance until it slithered away. 2) Climb back up the mountain that we just spent hours hiking and pray that when we came back it had retreated to its home. 3) Have Kate lay down on top of the snake and walk on her back like a plank. 4) Face the snake and jump higher than the best Olympic high jumper, clearing the snake. All jokes aside, there was only one option, because this snake was not moving. *Jump. Jump. Jump.*

As I grow older, I realize how important it is to be a person of action, so that's what I had to do. Taking a few lengthy steps back, I gained as much momentum as I could, cleared the creepy crawler and ran straight to the car upon landing, trusting Kate could make it back on her own.

In both stories, there were options: I could have let fear debilitate and destroy, or I could have trusted God and faced the fear head on. We could have stayed in our Airbnb all weekend knowing that someone could be waiting outside to murder us. We could have waited out the snake, which could've taken the whole day to move on. Instead, we faced fear together, walking out of the Airbnb and flying over the snake. If we didn't do those things, we never would have been able to get to the other side and see what God had planned for us past that fear. Sometimes when facing fear, you just have to run right at it and jump as high as you can, not looking back one bit. Put on your wings and fly.

If these examples don't seem too parallel to life, if they are too much of a stretch for you, I've got more. This trip, in and of itself, is a good example. I was afraid of going on this trip. I almost quit multiple times before the trip even started, due to fear. You have no idea how many people asked me the question, "Aren't you afraid?" They gave me a huge list of things to fear: getting murdered by a stranger, my car breaking down, running out of money, or not having a career when I came home. The number one fear people had for me was that I was going to get killed—and they were serious. I appreciate the love, but seriously? I was so excited and passionate about this trip and what God was doing, and it seemed people were trying to instill fear into me so I wouldn't go. That is not encouraging! But luckily, God made us all different so we can live our lives fully the way he wants us to.

I went on the trip. I made it through the whole thing, and it was undoubtedly the best experience of my life. God taught me so much. God showed up so much, blessing me with life experiences at the age of twenty-five that some people may never have in a lifetime. God used the trip to shape me more into the man I am today. He used the trip to inspire other people and bring other people hope. He used the trip to help other people grow in their faith!

Now, if I had let fear win, what would have happened? If I listened to my fear, I wouldn't have gone on this trip. I wouldn't have seen God work so much in my life. I wouldn't be nearly the person I am today, and I would have missed out on so much life. I wouldn't be writing a book right now.

To solidify the point, here is what God provided through Izzi.

Izzi was fearless. I wasn't. But fearlessness can be contagious. At Grand Tetons National Park, hiking Jenny Lake, Izzi helped me overcome my fear—not of snakes, but of heights. Izzi and I saw a huge rock about fifteen feet high overlooking the beautiful body of water. We approached it and before I could blink, Izzi was in the water, with a shivering, joyous smile on her face. Izzi, getting ready for round two, noticed I wasn't jumping in. I had never done anything like this before and I was scared.

After Izzi badgered me with encouragement and I remembered God's truth, "do not be afraid," I knew I had to face my fear. And so, I jumped.

Pure bliss. I didn't just jump into a freezing body of water in Wyoming—I faced a fear and felt completely liberated from the experience.

And guess what? In Washington and Oregon, *I* was the first one out of the two of us to jump into Colchuck Lake, and the only one to jump into Blue Pool. I essentially free climbed down to Blue Pool, which was actually extremely dangerous. One week after facing my fear with Izzi, I was taking the same fears (and more) head on. If I had never jumped into Jenny Lake with Izzi by my side, I don't know if I would have ever jumped into Colchuck or Blue Pool. If I had never faced that initial fear, I wouldn't have enjoyed some of the most blissful experiences of my life.

God gave us a brain and a healthy fear to protect us—the enemy only takes away. He tries—key word: *tries*—to debilitate and destroy the plans God has for us with unhealthy fear. But what does God say? Every day? *Do not be afraid.*

God has a beautiful, fruitful, bold life ahead for you. If you sit in fear, you may never be able to reap all that he has sown. You do not have to be afraid. And even if you are, you can face it with God, head on. Charge into it and through it. There is always something beautiful on the other side.

Before starting the next chapter, I want you to ponder this question: What would you do if you weren't afraid? Better yet, what could God possibly do in and through you if you lived a fearless life?

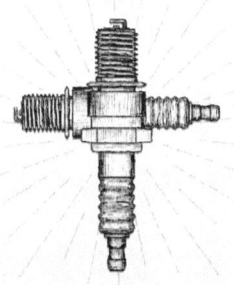

THE STATUE OF DAVID

June 22 to June 25, 2021 - Oregon
Days 27 through 30
July 12 to July 16, 2021 - Oklahoma
Days 47 through 51

August 30, 2020 was the most important day of my life. Not because I ran a half marathon that morning (which was pretty great—I even made the news), but because I decided to give my life to Jesus Christ. I felt a gravitational pull in my chest, calling me to get baptized. It was the most important day of my life. Though, that day, I don't think I understood the weight and magnitude of what had been done.

As Peter said, "Each of you must repent of your sins and turn to God, and be baptized in the name of Jesus Christ for the forgiveness of your sins. Then you will receive the gift of the Holy Spirit" (Acts 2:38, NLT).

I knew I had been baptized and had given my life to Christ, but there was a lot I did not understand. There still is. We will never know it all. There will always be questions, but I am learning that it is more about what and who we *do* know, not what we *don't* know.

So what do we know? We know that God loved the world so much, he gave his one and only son, so that everyone who believes in him will not perish but have eternal life (John 3:16, NLT). We know that even Jesus was baptized, knew the need for baptism, and was tempted by the devil (Matthew 3:13-17, NLT & Matthew 4:1-11, NLT). We know that Jesus will carry our burdens and give us rest in him (Matthew 11:28-30, NLT). We know we are supposed to make disciples of all nations, baptizing them in the name of the Father, the Son, and the Holy Spirit, while being sure to teach them the commands Jesus has given, knowing he is always with us (Matthew 28:18-20, NLT). We know that although we don't want to sin, sin is in us—but through this fleshly battle, we can have freedom because of Jesus Christ our Lord (Romans 7:14-25, NLT). We know that nothing, absolutely nothing can separate us from God's love (Romans 8:35-39, NLT). We know that if we believe in our hearts Jesus is Lord and that God raised him from the dead, and by openly declaring this, we will be saved (Romans 10:8-13, NLT). We know that God's grace is free and undeserved (Romans 11:6, NLT). And we know that Jesus is for everyone and wants everyone (Acts 34-36, NLT).

That is what scripture says. What scripture *doesn't* say is that upon baptism, you will be perfect and never sin again. It also doesn't say Jesus died a sinner's death, paying the ultimate sacrifice, so you have to carry weight and shame of every mistake you make. Or that the burdens in your life are yours to carry and yours alone, or that you are meant to isolate, crumble, and live a life of insecurity, pain, and loneliness. It does not say that we are not good enough for Jesus because we have sinned too much and messed up too much.

Those are all lies. Lies. Lies.

The sad truth is that me, many others in this world, and probably you have all believed lies such as these. Perhaps you still do.

God is a God of transformation. He will change you and transform you. He has the power to heal you and take away your temptations to sin instantly, but he also has the wisdom to let you choose him and choose freedom, learning and growing along the way. The hard but awesome truth is that he will do it however he wants, because he is that cool of a God.

He died for everyone so that those who receive his new life will no longer live for themselves. Instead they will live for Christ, who died and was raised for them. So we have stopped evaluating others from a human point of view. At one time we thought of Christ as merely from a human point of view. How differently we know him now! This means that anyone who belongs to Christ has become a new person. The old life is gone; a new me has begun. (2 Corinthians 5:15-17, NLT)

> When I went under the water, completely surrendering my heart and soul to Jesus, I arose with him. My old life was gone and my new life with Christ in me had begun. I was free. This was completely true, but what I didn't quite understand is that freedom didn't mean perfection. Quite the opposite.

Freedom meant accepting Jesus, knowing I am imperfect, and dying to myself daily, while picking up my cross and following Jesus. That is where you find the true freedom in him—in accepting and following Jesus, clinging onto him like there's no tomorrow, and throwing down your old self. And what is another word for "throwing down your old self?" Repentance.

Simply, to turn from sin—or one's old life—and seek the new life Christ has for them.

Jesus died so we could truly know him, see ourselves the way he does, and feel his never-ending love for us. He died so we could experience freedom through him, both now on this earth and later in heaven. All we have to do is repent, believe, and accept this truth, and we will achieve freedom. We just have to remember that freedom is not perfection, because we will never be perfect.

God is a refiner, just like Michaelangelo. *The Statue of David,* one of Michaelangelo's finest pieces of art, took time. It started as a slab and had to be chiseled over and over, time and time again, until the masterpiece was finally done. And although *The Statue of David* is an amazing piece of art, I guarantee it doesn't have a five-star Yelp review. People will find something wrong with it, because people are critics. But it is a masterpiece, and it is perfect to its creator.

Did you know that we are God's masterpiece?

God saved you by his grace when you believed. And you can't take credit for this: it is a gift from God. Salvation is not a reward for the good things we have done, so none of us can boast about it. For we are God's masterpiece. He has created us anew in Christ Jesus, so we can do good things he planned for us long ago. (Ephesians 2:8-10, NLT)

We are a masterpiece to God. We are perfect to him, our creator, and although he is always chiseling us and we will never be perfect, he still will always love us and have a seat for us in heaven because of his son, Jesus Christ.

Now, let's put all of this into context. I am a sinner, but I am saved by grace, and because of that, I do not own that I am a sinner. I am adopted, redeemed, a child of God—I am no longer a sinner. I have sinned, and I still do fall into sin, but because of Jesus, my identity is not that of a sinner. My identity is that of a loved child of God.

Some of the sins I have struggled with or still struggle with today range from lustfulness, pride, selfishness, cussing, gambling, partying—you name it. Although I will never be perfect, I am always being refined by my creator.

How does this refining work? Well, here is how it has worked in my life. Before the trip, God had already been chiseling away pretty hard. I was the guy with endless stories from college and my early twenties about getting too drunk to remember much at all. The things I did remember were "legendary," and the things

I found out later I had done when I had no control over myself were "funny." The stories where something happened with a girl were bonus points. I was that guy. Before I got baptized, when I was starting to go to church again, I once had to sit on the end row because I was certain I would throw up from being hungover. Plus, I coached baseball. I coached fifteen-year-olds to multiple State Championships, and I thought a good way to motivate them was with the occasional cuss word. I thought as long as I was not directing it at them, it was appropriate. I was that guy.

Thank God he is *The Guy*. Between getting baptized and going on this trip, God refined me in these areas so much. Here's how it happened: I would go out and drink, as usual. I would kiss a girl I was not pursuing. I would swear for no reason. But then, I would feel an internal feeling that what I was doing was not right.

Before giving my life to Christ, God had been pulling at my heart for quite a while. I had grown to know these things were wrong—I even realized how much they negatively affected me— but they became coping mechanisms that led into a deeper pit. They drove me to severe anxiety and depression.

Once I gave my life to Christ, it was a different kind of "wrong" feeling. It was from God. It was like a parent telling me, "Son, this isn't healthy for you. This isn't what is best for you. There is a different route I have planned for you that is full of life. Stop searching for these things."

This is what I call conviction, and it is quite a beautiful feeling. It is God working in your heart, telling you that he wants better for you. Because he loves you, he desires for you to listen to that gut feeling and pursue him, instead.

For me, it was this part of my journey where the road trip came in.

God had done so much work in my life and changed me so much. It was an amazing feeling. I was living freely with him, daily—until I fell. During the trip, on multiple occasions I had made decisions to do what felt right or fun in the moment, even if I knew God had already convicted me of what I was doing. There were times I "stumbled" and immediately felt horrible. I knew what I was doing was wrong, but still had a lack of self-control. There was a horrid, wretched feeling in me, but this one wasn't conviction—it was *hardcore shame.*

I heard Shawn Johnson of Red Rocks Church give a sermon on shame vs. guilt or conviction. This is what I gathered from him: guilt, or conviction, is "I did something wrong or bad." Shame is "I am wrong or bad." Shame is exactly what I felt. "How can I be a man of God when I just did that? I don't deserve God's love and grace and forgiveness. I am unworthy." These thoughts and more raided my mind a mile a minute. Then, there is what follows; when I feel shame, I shut down and isolate myself. I take a step back and believe all the lies.

Hear me: shame is not from God or of God. Shame is from the enemy. We do not have to feel or sit in shame. That's what the enemy wants. *Conviction inspires you to change* and be a better man or woman of God. Shame makes you feel worthless and tries to keep you sitting in it, until you believe all the lies and spiral out of control. Shame has no place in your life. You may have messed up, but you are not messed up. You still are God's masterpiece.

You might now be asking, if God is refining me over time, always offering me grace and mercy, and sees me as his beautiful masterpiece, is it okay to sin? Should I hold on to that part of my life? The answer: absolutely not! Jesus died *not* for us to take advantage of his grace and mercy; Jesus died so we could live a new creation in full relation with him, with our hearts fully surrendered.

Jesus offers freedom right now, but to have that freedom we need to hold on to him daily, and let go of our old selves daily—something that I don't always do, because I am not perfect.

And even if you are trying to "get rid of this sin," how are you doing that? Are you trying to stop sinning just by telling yourself not to do this sin everyday? Because I have fallen into that trap. There is only one real solution: Jesus. Focus on your savior, not your sin.

Savior. Not sin.

Drop or turn away from your old self daily, pick up Jesus daily, and don't let go. I have an all-too-embarrassing story to share that will complete this analogy.

On this trip, my diet was extremely poor. I drove a lot of miles, often spending whole days in my car driving, and every day that I was driving from one place to another, this is what was riding shotgun: a loaf of bread, peanut butter, Cuties, Slim Jims, Arizona Iced Tea, and Sour Patch Kids. When I wasn't eating meals in my car, I would eat whatever the opportunity provided.

Now, we are all human, but at twenty-seven, I am still not comfy talking about this with other people—especially women. But we all poop. Some girls say they don't poop, or they don't until they're married, but I don't buy it. This topic might be uncomfortable, but let's just get comfy with it, since that's where the story is going. God created us all this way. Stop judging. Remove that log from your eye. (Matthew 7:1-6, NLT)

Karissa, Kaykay, and I were traveling from Washington to Oregon. Since our paths were eventually going to divert, we were in two separate cars. I was trailing them as we were headed to our next campsite, which was a few hours away. Rolling down the beautiful Oregon roads, I got that urge—you know, the, *I have eaten too many Slim Jims* urge. After thirty minutes of waiting for a rest stop, it became quite unbearable.

As beautiful as the Pacific Northwest is, they should really invest in some better cell phone towers. With essentially no service to pull up a map on my phone, I was losing hope for an upcoming rest stop.

When you don't know what else to do, what else is there to do? Pray. "God, please, please, please, please bring a restroom soon. *Please!*" It got to the point where I knew what God wanted me to do: be the person he created me to be and indulge in the nature he created.

I pulled over quickly, praying Karissa and Kaykay wouldn't stop their car to see what I was doing. I ran into the beautiful forest, hid behind a tree fifty times my size, and worked on my squat form. "Keep your knees behind your toes," I thought as I dropped off something in the woods. Freaking out, hoping that the cars that drove by in that forty-five second window didn't see the man behind the tree, I sprinted back to the car.

Hands on the wheel, it was time to go catch up with the girls. When I gripped the wheel, I noticed something sticky all over my right hand. Yes, I leaned against the tree with my right hand for balance and, yes, I then was introduced to Oregon tree sap.

Sap aside, here's the deal: after dropping off that gift in the woods, I felt much lighter. I felt no more stress or anxiety about this situation—I felt like a new, confident, free man—with sticky hands.

Back to Jesus. This is exactly what we have been talking about. Dying to your old self daily. Or "letting go" of the weight you have been carrying around. Dropping off the old you and leaving it behind. And then what? Going straight to Jesus, "being stuck" to Jesus because you are so glued to him and your relationship with him. You don't have to hold on to your sins. You don't have to live the life of "your old self." You are a new creation in Christ. Cling to him like tree sap and let go of your past self like a bowel movement.

In weirdest terms possible, that is the Gospel. Jesus died for every single one of us. We all will always fall short, but because of his sacrifice, we have new life. Because of Jesus, we can be free, right here, right now. The Gospel itself is perfect. Jesus is perfect. Just remember, the Gospel doesn't mean *we* are perfect. It means the opposite. We are imperfect people in need of a perfect savior.

When Jesus heard this, he said, "Healthy people don't need a doctor—sick people do." Then he added, "Now go and learn the meaning of this Scripture: 'I want you to show mercy, not offer sacrifices.' For I have come to call not those who think they are righteous, but those who know they are sinners"

It is knowing that we fall short and acknowledging our need for a savior—the savior, *The Spark Plug*—that we can be saved.

In Oklahoma, there was a fall—maybe the biggest fall of the whole trip. On this part of the trip, I was alone for multiple days and able to explore Tulsa. We know how much I love rollerblading, so I had to check out the local trail system. I would rate it a 5.42/10. It was okay. But the local skate park I found was a solid 8.72/10. It was *gnarly*.

Prior to this skate park visit, the last time I had "shred the gnar" I was probably twelve years old. Luckily, being twenty-five, my brain still hadn't developed much since then and I still was flirting with that "healthy fear" we talked about. I was having a blast, coasting all around and giving head nods out to the teenagers there, until there was another type of blast—a blast that fortunately did not end in any broken bones, but easily could have.

I was trying to be cool and video myself for a TikTok when my legs decided to go incognito and my whole body slammed down. I was dropped down, off a three-foot ramp. It was such a hard fall—I have video evidence of me sounding like a dying old man who had the wind knocked out of him, grunting choice cuss words. (As mentioned, refining is always happening.)

But you know what? Even though I felt like I broke my back and fractured my lumbar—I got back up. The same is true for us on our journey with Jesus. Knowing that we aren't perfect and that we still may fall sometimes into temptation and sin, we can get back up with Jesus, every time.

"The godly may trip seven times, but they will get up again" (Proverbs)

We aren't perfect. We never will be. We will fall. We will always have plenty of room for chiseling in our lives. We will never come near the real *Statue of David*. We are probably a lot more fat-looking statues compared to David, who *still* isn't perfect. But that is the point. Jesus came for us, just as we are. He came for me. He came for you. He loves us and just wants our hearts. In him, we are new creations, and because he chose us, we get to choose him and the new life, every. Single. Day.

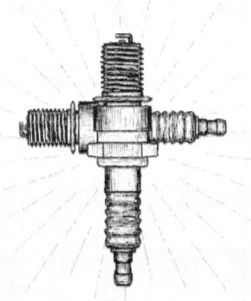

PEOPLE

od created the heavens and earth, light, the sky, land, food, animals, and yes, people. He created us so carefully and intricately. What an interesting creation.

You made all the delicate, inner parts of my body and knit me together in my mother's womb. Thank you for making me so wonderfully complex! Your workmanship is marvelous– how well I know it. (Psalm 139:13-14, NLT)

David says it in the Psalm above: we are so wonderfully complex! And we really are, aren't we? We are made so wonderfully complex, and we also have a really easy time making things in life even more complex. We create divisions within each other and we turn our shoulders to someone just because we think differently than them, yet we all desperately need each other. Without other humans, we would go crazy.

What if Eve had never been created and Adam was alone? He never would have procreated and would have been alone for a lifetime. What if you were the only person on this earth? I don't care what you tell me, you would go crazy. We have all seen *Cast Away* with Tom Hanks. The dude went crazy, and so would we.

People make life complicated, but we desperately need other people, and they need us. Sounds like I'm making things complex, I know. But I'm not. It's really quite simple.

Both Jesus and Paul surrounded themselves with all people—and when I say "all people," I mean *all* people. Neither of them secluded themselves in a certain group or strayed away from encounters with people who were "different." In fact, they leaned into those opportunities. They gave everyone a chance—everyone.

However, we humans, especially Christians, tend to not to surround ourselves with someone because they are "different" or not living a "righteous life." Because they are out partying, smoking, having sex, stealing, or whatever else. We decide to surround ourselves with only other Christians.

On the flip side, we may give our lives to Christ but not seek a Christian community. We decide to keep doing life only with the people we were doing life with before, and we still partake in the activities that "we died to" when we were baptized.

I don't think either is right. Jesus and Paul both laid out simple paths of what *is* right, and how we are supposed to live simply, with other people.

There are patterns common to these men and their encounters with other people. The one that sticks out to me is that they both spread love and did it boldly.

Nowhere in the Bible does Jesus say "I love you" to anyone. That's pretty powerful, because so many people preach that Jesus loves you—and they are absolutely correct, he does. But how do we know that, if not by his words? *By his actions.* Jesus loved. He didn't have to say it, because he showed it everywhere he went to everyone he encountered, even when he was on the cross—especially when he was on the cross. Paul shared love boldly, too. Throughout the whole book of Acts, he showed his love in the fact that he was sharing the one who encompasses love. He was sharing Jesus, boldly, everywhere he went to everyone.

Paul and Jesus also both had circles that loved them and encouraged them, as they also encouraged their circles. When I say "circles," I mean a close-knit group of people to live together with God in the center. Jesus had twelve disciples. Paul was always traveling with someone—whether Barnabas or Silas, he had a brother in Christ who was walking alongside him.

Another strong theme is believers encouraging believers. It seems that almost everywhere Paul goes, he is sharing with believers and encouraging them, or vice versa.

There was an instance where a mob stoned Paul, thinking he was dead—but believers were there, and guess what? He lived.

They stoned Paul and dragged him out of town, thinking he was dead. But as the believers gathered around him, he got up and went back into the town. The next day he left with Barnabas for Derbe. (Acts 14:19b-20, NLT)

Think about how powerful that is. Paul was thought to be dead. Believers gathered around him. He wasn't dead. He was left for dead, but believers gathered around him. And he was back at it the next day! Not even a day off for TLC (tender love and care).

There have been times where I have felt like I was spiritually dying, but I had believers gathering around me. And I got back up.

There have also been times where I have felt down and didn't surround myself with believers. In those times, I wanted to stay down.

Jesus and Paul loved everyone well, and they also had a great community of believers around them to be encouraged. What else? They spent time with people who *didn't* believe. That is the whole point.

Jesus came and told his disciples, "I have been given all authority in heaven and on earth. Therefore, go and make disciples of all nations, baptizing them in the name of the Father and the Son and the Holy Spirit" (Matthew 28:19, NLT).

The point is to share Jesus and be a vessel to help grow his Kingdom. Jesus spent time with people who had sinned, but he didn't partake in sin with them. He loved them, with the hope in his heart that they would follow him. Paul shared Jesus everywhere he went. He shared with everyone in hopes that they would believe and be baptized. Some didn't, and Paul moved on, continuing his mission.

Both of these guys understood the importance of loving people—all people. They understood the importance of being firm in who they were and what they believed, while loving others. They understood the importance of being surrounded by others who loved them and encouraged them.

Learning from these two guys, I believe I am supposed to love everyone. I believe I am supposed to hang out with anyone and everyone. While hanging out with everyone, I must be firm in who I am and what I believe, hoping that they can see Jesus in me and desire him. And I believe I need love and encouragement from those in my circle.

The love that is poured into you is the love that will be poured out from you.

When I went hot tubbing last night with my pastor for a couple hours, we discussed how our walk with God and life is going, and we prayed together. I felt love and life poured into me. Then, when I exited the hot tub and saw I had received a text from a great friend about desiring to grow in his relationship with God, I was able to pour life and love into my friend. I was encouraged by someone in my circle, so I then could encourage another in my circle. It is a cycle, and it's beautiful. It points out our need for God, for his love, and the community he provides, so we can be bold in him wherever we go, with whoever we encounter.

OLD TIES, NEW FAITH

June 8 to June 11, 2021 - Idaho
Days 13 through 16

The first night in Boise, Idaho, was spent on a solo hike to a place called "Table Rock." Table Rock is a beautiful lookout above the city. At the overlook is a giant cross—a perfect place to spend a moment with God and reflect before meeting one of my former players from when I coached college baseball. That night, I went out for sushi with a lanky pitcher named Jake.

The raw fish was great, but the raw conversation was even better. A topic came up that I truly never thought would enter the picture with Jake: Jesus. Two years prior, when I was coaching Jake, these conversations didn't happen. The unexpected topic of Jesus arising opened the door to another level of conversation. Things are always enhanced when *The Spark Plug's* in the center. Jake and I both shared the testimony of Jesus in our lives over the past two years. Turns out, God had taken both of our worlds, flipped them upside down, and changed our lives for the better. It was so unexpected and encouraging.

When I left dinner to go meet my new friend, Morgan, it was no surprise I was encouraged and full of life. Being encouraged and full of life led to cartwheels in front of the Boise State football stadium, enjoying delicious local ice cream, and most importantly, sharing my testimony with Morgan.

I didn't know Morgan's faith background. I didn't need to. I was supposed to be on this trip with whoever God put in my path.

The worst thing I could have done while screening for this trip was ask each person if they were a Christian. The other worst thing I could've done is asked people if they were willing to go party and rage and have a fun time. The best thing I could've done is waited to see who God put in my path and then committed to loving them the best I could, leading with Jesus and sharing him.

Because of my encounter with my fellow brother in Christ, I was freshly encouraged. So when God inevitably opened the door to share with Morgan, she was going to hear what God had done in my life. What is poured in, will be poured out.

JOY AND JOELLE

Receiving encouragement from those in our circle is awesome, but that is not the only purpose to having those people in your life. Accountability and challenging questions or conversations, done in love, is another. I can't even imagine how many tough conversations Jesus and his disciples had which were no doubt hard to hear, but done in love only.

May 2, 2021 - South Dakota
25 days prior to the road trip

Joelle kicked it off. Joelle, my good friend from back home, asked me some challenging questions before the trip while we were rollerblading—yes, while we were rollerblading! Talk about killing the good vibes, Joelle. Regardless, it was needed. Joelle proposed two questions about the journey ahead: 1) "Aren't you worried financially?" and 2) "You are staying with an awful lot of girls on this trip. Aren't you worried about falling into temptation?"

Good questions, Joelle. Good questions that were instantly received by a giant wall of defense mechanisms. It was a pretty short conversation because I did not have much to say other than that I believed God would provide financially and that I would not fall into the trap of temptation. Oh, the ego.

Although I didn't appreciate her challenge in the moment, I needed it. She wasn't trying to make me feel doubt. She was making sure I was being wise and protecting myself, my heart, and others. She was loving and caring for her friend, while being real with them. We all need a Joelle. And at times, we may have to be the Joelle for others.

June 30 to July 3, 2021 - California
Days 35 through 38

Back on the trip, Joy—my TikTok wedding date—hosted me in Orange County, California. The itinerary was jam-packed for a few days. We had rooftop dinners, saw MMA champ Conor McGregor ride his bike alongside the coast (California is crazy), spent a whole day at the local theme park, saw the Hollywood sign, strutted down Hollywood Boulevard, and ate In-N-Out (another controversial burger chain) while driving through Malibu and listening to "Malibu" by Miley Cyrus. We also attended a worship night, had a night drive by Huntington Beach, and ended it all with a Fourth of July party. Jam-packed, as I told you. We even took the time to watch *La La Land* with my lookalike, Ryan Gosling. But through all the amazing time spent with Joy, there was one conversation that stuck out.

On my final day with Joy, walking along the beach, I couldn't wait to tell her how I was so excited to move to Colorado after my trip. I absolutely fell in love with Colorado while on my trip. Barb, Kate, and company were some great salespeople, although they didn't have to say much. The mountains spoke for themselves. Either way, I was certain after this trip that I would reside in Colorado.

Joy, being the good, loving friend she is, called me on my future plans. She didn't say I wouldn't move to Colorado; she just questioned if I was sure that God was calling me there. She asked if I was truly trusting God with my plan or if I was making the plan myself. If only she knew how to break through my internal Great Wall of China…with that barrier up, it was another short conversation, where I spoke few words.

Here we are, three years later, and I still do not reside in Colorado. God had different plans. I have since admitted to Joy she was wiser than me, and still is.

It was hard to hear Joelle and Joy's challenging thoughts and questions, but upon reflection, I am so thankful for them and their hearts. These people loved me enough to ask hard questions I probably wasn't ready for, questions that led to conviction from the Lord. Questions that led to maturation and life change. The people in your circle are extremely important.

They say we are a combination of the five people we spend the most time with. If you are wise, you will spend a lot of time with people like Joelle and Joy.

HANNA ROZE

Hanna Roze is an amazing woman who was one of the most influential people on my trip. Like Barb and Kate, Hanna was a rock. Every single time I drove from state to state, as routine as the morning paper, Hanna Roze and I would have a phone call. These phone calls varied in length. Sometimes they lasted only seconds. Sometimes minutes. Sometimes hours. Sometimes we would be complete dorks and make fun of her dumb cat, Milo. Sometimes we would share our dreams and aspirations. Other times, we would encourage each other with Christ in the center. I needed Hanna to get through this trip, and she was always there for me, no matter what.

The funny thing is, although Hanna was there for me the whole duration of the trip, I didn't visit her. In fact, I didn't meet Hanna until after the trip was over. Hanna and I met on TikTok. Commenting on each other's posts led to a direct message, which led to a phone call, which led to becoming best friends over FaceTime.

The story of how we met in person is actually pretty awesome. Hannah flew from Northern California to South Dakota to be my wedding date a few months after the trip. Yes, I have had three wedding dates in my life with people I met on TikTok. This might be the world record. Hanna flew to South Dakota just to hang out with me, her friend she had never met before in person, for the weekend. I think this shows the kind of heart that Hanna has. Hanna is the kind of soul who still mails handwritten letters to express her love and gratitude, when the rest of the world resorts to text messages if you're lucky. We need more Hannas today, if you ask me.

Hanna has an extreme ability to encourage and pour love into her friends, so they can, in turn, pour love out to others. Specifically, the love of Jesus.

Bouncing over to the east coast, twenty-four states into my adventure, I had a choice to make: explore Florida and South Carolina by myself for seven days, or go home. People had backed out last minute, and with no plan and nowhere to stay, feeling burned out, I decided to fly home for a week. When I was home, I had time to engage in my community for an evening at a local church. It was amazing to catch up with people I hadn't seen in two months and enjoy the early August evening, while destroying my unathletic Christian friends in kickball.

That night I met a girl who had me "smitten." Let's call her Grace. The next evening, we went on a date. Two nights later, another date. I liked her. A lot. Unfortunately, it was time to fly back to Jacksonville, Florida and venture through another twenty-four states. Grace and I decided we would communicate while I was away and pursue dating when I returned.

Remember, we agreed that I was definitely not ready for a relationship. The next couple weeks of the trip, Grace was on my mind. A lot. Too much. So when Grace started not responding to my texts or calls when I was in the upper northeast part of the country, I began to struggle. Feeling rejected and not knowing why is hard—this is why we find our identity and fulfillment in *The Spark Plug*, not other people.

Having not heard from Grace in days, I gave her space. At the same time, a day before arriving in Delaware, the person meant to host me texted that they would not be able to after all. Now, not only was the girl I was pursuing me ghosting me, the person who I was supposed to explore Wilmington, DE with also doesn't want to spend time with me.

Finding an Airbnb last minute in suburban Delaware, I realized this time alone was exactly what God had planned. When I finally received a page-long text from Grace telling me that it wasn't going to work out, without any explanation of why, I needed to be alone. Lying in my upstairs bedroom, wallowing in pity and isolating, the phone rang. *Hanna Roze.*

She stayed on the phone with me for hours. She reminded me of my worth and value, of God's love and plan for me and my life, and even had us take out our Bibles. She pointed me to the truth. That's who Hanna is, someone who can point you to Christ, remind you of who you are in him, and guide you to the real encouragement to be found in *The Spark Plug*.

Hanna was there for me the whole time, and I know she still is today. Hanna's constant love, encouragement, and pointing to Christ—along with many other people along the way—is the only reason I was able to not just finish this trip, but also share Jesus along the way.

MARY IN MICHIGAN

September 6 to September 8, 2021 - Michigan
Days 103 through 105

All that encouragement, love, and pointing me toward Jesus allowed me to have the boldness and confidence to share him in Michigan—the home of Mary and her college roommates.

Mary and her friends allowed me to stay in their apartment with them. One of Mary's friends, Brooke, was celebrating her 21st birthday the weekend I was there. They had the festivities all lined up: a weekend of partying and doing things the old me loved to do. Chugging beers, playing beer pong, and indulging in drinking games.

This is where the conflict comes in. We must let go of our old lives, like a poop in the woods, and cling on to Christ, daily. God had done a bunch of refining in my life in the area of alcohol. I had those convictions in my life already and did not desire to become drunk anymore, knowing there was a good chance I would not glorify God when I was in a state of "no control."

I knew that I was meant to spend this weekend with Mary and her friends in Michigan. I was meant to love them and show them the love of Jesus. I was meant to spend time with them. I was also meant to stand firm in who I was and what I believed.

Brooke was excited to celebrate her 21st birthday. It is a special day in our lives, the day we are finally "legal." Mary, Brooke, and their friends were ready for a fun night celebrating. We ventured downtown, started with a meal, then progressed to the drinks.

Here is the cool thing: because I am a child of God, because I am a Christian, this doesn't mean I have to never sip alcohol again in my life. What it does mean is God had convicted me and refined me in the area of drinking to the point that I am comfortable having a drink or two, knowing I will have the discernment to stop and still be able to bring glory to him.

He has changed my heart. They say you don't have to change your life before you give your life to God, that you don't have to be "sober" or "fixed." Duh! That's the point! You go to him and he does all the hard work! He does the refining, he choreographs the heart change!

Because of this, I was able to enjoy a few drinks with Mary, Brooke, and their other friends, before switching to Blue Dolphins (a.k.a., water). The girls probably had a little too much to drink. With the effects of some shots taking over, Mary became over emotional upon arriving home. As tears streamed down Mary's face, her friends urged me to go straight upstairs to my guest bedroom while they handled the situation.

One hour later, Mary knocked on my door. She unnecessarily apologized for crying. Other than reassuring her that we all cry, and it was okay, I told her I desired to know her heart.

We dove into conversation and Mary very vulnerably shared with me that she was struggling with the memory, or lack thereof, of a very traumatic event from her past. It hurt my heart to know what she had been through, but I know someone who could help.

It wasn't long into our conversation that I felt led to mention *The Spark Plug.*

That's when the conversation came to life. We talked about Jesus, the life he has to offer, how he sees her, her identity in him, and the freedom found in him. According to my journal, we talked till 3 a.m. That's when Mary called her sister, then and there, and told her this: "I just talked to this guy about Jesus and it was amazing! I talked to my friends for an hour before and nothing they said helped, but now I feel so much better."

That is the power of *The Spark Plug.* The power to insert himself into the situations that seem the most helpless and hopeless. When nothing else will bring you through, Jesus will, and he will give you life—so much life that you have to call your sister at 3 a.m. and tell her all about it.

The beautiful thing is that I did nothing here. Jesus brought forth the opportunity and divinely created that moment; I just was obedient in sharing what he had done in my life. He is the one who divinely placed Hanna, Barb, Kate, and everyone else in my circle. So thank God for opportunities. Thank God for Hanna Roze. Thank God for Mary and Michigan. Really, thank God for God.

People. Are we supposed to love only certain people? No. Are we supposed to live like all people? No. People are meant to love people with encouragement, accountability, and life. People need people. People need life. And what is life? True life?

> Jesus spoke to the people once more and said, "I am the light of the world. If you follow me, you won't have to walk in darkness, because you will have the light that leads to life" (John)
>
> Jesus is life. People need life. People need *The Spark Plug*—Jesus.

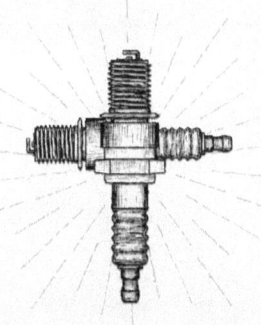

NAKEDNESS

July 3 to July 6, 2021 - California
Days 38 through 41

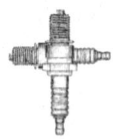

I sleep naked. That's right, fully nude.

I haven't done this my whole life; I tried it once in high school and thought it was a little uncomfortable, but gave it another try about a year ago. I have grown to love it. It is freeing. In the privacy of my room, the security of my home, I can completely just be me, naked. It is such a freeing and comfortable feeling… except for that one time my roommate sleepwalked into my room at six in the morning. That was a little uncomfortable.

While on the topic of nakedness, let's talk about the first book in the Bible, Genesis. Adam and Eve were created beautifully, in the image of God. That is how we humans are created: in the image of God.

> "So God created human beings in his own image.
> In the image of God he created them, male and
> female he created them" (Genesis 1:27, NLT).

Shortly after humans were created in God's image, we sinned.

> The woman was convinced. She saw that the tree
> was beautiful and its fruit looked delicious, and she
> wanted the wisdom it would give her. So she took
> some of the fruit and ate it. Then she gave some
> to her husband, who was with her, and he ate it
> too. At that moment their eyes were opened, and

they suddenly felt shame at their nakedness. So
they sewed fig leaves together to cover themselves.
(Genesis 3:6-7, NLT)

You mean to tell me we were created in God's image, naked, with
no shame? Humans were literally naked and felt no embarrassment
or shame. Man, that is a hard concept to accept today. Being naked
in front of others—maybe even in front of ourselves in a mirror—to
some, can be one of the most embarrassing and shameful things
that we can feel in our world today.

Maybe that's why when we do big speeches, they tell us to
imagine everyone else naked—if everyone else is naked, they must
feel embarrassed and insecure, which makes us more confident
because of their lack of confidence.

Today, the more layers we show of ourselves—physically,
emotionally, spiritually—the more naked we feel, and the more
insecure we tend to become. But we were *created in God's image,
naked*. We were created to be seen for who we truly are, physically,
emotionally, and spiritually. We were created to be the true versions
of ourselves, the versions that were created in God's image.

This is something I struggle with today—being my true self.
The true Stephen God created me to be. I can be extremely insecure,
and the more layers I show of myself, the easier it is to overthink
and be afraid of what others think. Whether it is my looks, my
thoughts, my faith, my actions—I sometimes let my insecurities
hold me back from being exactly who God created me to be.

Writing this is hard because God created me. He made me
perfect. I am his son. He intricately made me exactly how I am
supposed to be. He gave me the tools and gifts I have for his
Kingdom. Yet, sometimes I choose to not dive into that, simply
because I am worried about others seeing the real, true Stephen.

When I was a kid, I was the person that God created me to be. In September, 2020, my mom wrote me a card reminding me of who I was when I was younger. It read, "I am so proud of you. Your whole life you have brought great joy into my heart. You have always been just you and not afraid to be you. You wore the same tiki orange shirt day after day. You never took off your skateboard helmet for six months. You mismatched your converse shoes—you are perfect when you do you."

She hit the nail on the head. "Me doing me" is me being who God created me to be, in his perfect image.

In reality though, I haven't "always been just me and not afraid to be me." When I was growing up, that was true. But when I was in high school, I definitely worried about what others thought of me. After being introduced to materialism, comparison, and social media, it has been hard not to be more insecure the older I get.

You would like to think the older you are, the easier it gets, but that's not always the case. I wish we always thought like we did when we were kids—and I believe Jesus wishes this, too. Little children are fearless, they have hope, faith, and belief in things they cannot see. They are always trying new things. They say things that they "shouldn't say." They are humble and completely rely on their parents. They don't worry about what others think about them. They love anybody and everybody. They even run around naked from time to time, without a care in the world, because they are completely them, created in God's image. They haven't felt the shame of nakedness yet.

My third and final stop in California was with Amanda. I left Los Angeles with Joy and her friends on the evening of July third so I could enjoy the Fourth of July with Amanda in the San Diego area.

Amanda and I ventured to her family friend's house to celebrate America's Independence Day. Amanda had been celebrating the Fourth with this family ever since she was a child. Meeting a whole family of nine—brothers and sisters and their girlfriends and boyfriends and parents—was overwhelming.

As a kid, I loved being in large groups of people. As an adult, not so much—it is an easy road toward insecurity for me. So even before getting to know anyone there and having real conversations, I already felt insecure. It was really easy to tell myself the narrative that I was some kid from South Dakota who was crazy about Jesus and didn't fit in with these California kids. It was really easy to believe that narrative, and so I did.

I was really quiet. They probably thought I was super introverted, but no, I was just insecure. I was thinking about what they thought about me, my actions, my looks, how I talked, my faith. These people didn't even know me. They probably didn't care one lick about who I was, and probably didn't spend even seconds judging me, but I believed the lies and felt the shame and nakedness.

Everybody else, meanwhile, was having a blast—jumping into the pool, joking around, sipping drinks, and playing a game called "beer die." They were celebrating appropriately.

Now, I don't know if they noticed me being "in my head," but before long, the guys invited me to join them in playing beer die.

The premise: you have a long, rectangular, table. There are two players on each side. You throw a die super high up and try to land it in one of their cups on the corners of the table. There were other factors, such as being able to kick dice to your partner and stuff, but I honestly don't remember it all. I just remember what came from playing this game.

Before the game, the brothers who lived there made sure to tell me the house rules, which were simple: if you don't score one point for your team, you have to streak around the house—naked, twice—and finish your laps by jumping into the pool.

"Okay," I thought. "How hard can it be?"

Well.

I should have thought more.

As a coach, I know that always, *always*, athletes perform best when they are confident in themselves. Confidence and security go hand in hand, and therefore, so does success. If that's the case, then insecurity goes hand in hand with lacking confidence, and therefore, a higher chance of failing. Well, I was still feeling insecure. In other words, I wasn't feeling comfortable in my own skin. I wasn't comfortable showing the true, fun, excitable, competitive guy I am to these strangers.

And because of that, I paid the price. Feeling more and more pressure after every toss, still having not scored any points minutes into the game, I became quite nervous. Was I really going to have to streak in these strangers' backyard? The answer: yes. Yes, I was. I did not contribute one point to my team. Not one single point.

With all the testosterone flowing, the other twenty-year-old dudes couldn't help but be weirdly excited for what was about to happen. Someone they had just met was about to go streaking in their backyard, and they were going to watch.

I wanted to back down. I wanted to say no. But in this circumstance, I am glad I gave into the peer pressure. Sometimes, sometimes peer pressure can be good. And let's be honest, it's house rules. You can't disrespect that.

Respectfully, and thankfully, the girls went inside and the four men started to cheer and banter. It was time. Bottoms down. Like Adam and Eve using fig leaves, I equipped my hands to cover up. The race began. The naked race.

Those two laps were actually *awesome*. Rounding each corner of the backyard like I was rounding third base headed toward home, I felt free. Releasing my hands, doing the most memorable cannonball of my life, I was *really, really free.*

Greeted with a towel and my trunks, I had a revelation. After being insecure the whole day, this was the most secure I had felt. All the people around me laughing hysterically with disbelief that I actually did it, made me comfortable and secure.

That was the most confident, secure, and comfortable I felt that whole portion of the trip. I was fully seen, fully known, fully me, and felt fully liberated.

So what is the point here? Is everyone supposed to walk around naked because it is more freeing? Not exactly. That would be very illegal. But, we are supposed to be the most naked, real, raw versions of ourselves. We are supposed to be the ones who God created in his own image. When I was fully naked in front of those people, I was fully secure. That is how God made us, completely us and completely secure in him, because we are made in his image! He created us exactly how we are supposed to be. Don't miss this. Shame came from when we first ever sinned—and who did it come from? The serpent! Not from God. God never intended for us to feel shame. He never intended for us to feel insecure or to have to worry about who we are, what people think of us, our actions, our words, our beliefs.

He created us to live an amazing and beautiful life, in him and through him. And he still desires that for us! Jesus did not come down to earth and sacrifice himself so we could feel the weight of sin that Adam and Eve felt in that moment. *The Spark Plug* came down so we could feel free and secure, being exactly who God created us to be: naked and in his image.

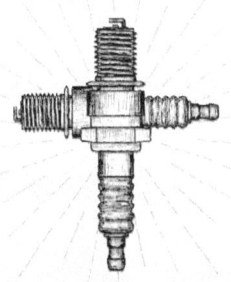

HIDDEN
IMMUNITY
IDOL

August 17 to August 20, 2021 - West Virginia
Days 83 through 86

I f you haven't watched the reality TV show *Survivor*, you need to check it out. They put eighteen people from all different walks of life somewhere in the wilderness, where they have to survive for twenty-six days. They have to complete physical challenges to earn rewards and even immunity—immunity means you cannot be voted out of the show, which happens once every episode.

This is a physical game, yes, but also an extremely social one. You want to build alliances that you trust will not deceive you, although there is only one winner. So, in order to win the title of "Sole Survivor," you will most likely have to deceive someone within your alliance to go further than them—but you don't want to "burn the bridge," because they may be on the jury at the end of the game (the group that ultimately votes for the winner out of the final three contestants). It is an extremely complex game and I desire to play it one day. Jeff Probst, if you are reading this, let's make it happen.

A very interesting twist in *Survivor* is that there is more than one way to gain immunity and be safe from a vote. Other than winning an immunity challenge, there are hidden "immunity idols." Immunity idols are very rare. They can only be used for one individual, and make it so that person cannot be voted out when used. They give the player so much power. Most of the time, if a player has an immunity idol, their odds of making it further in the game—and even winning, are multiplied.

This is all great, if the player can find an idol. The hard thing about the hidden immunity idol is exactly that: it is hidden. In the middle of the jungle. Normally, it is a very small medallion or bracelet hidden in a very large place. It is about as close as you can get to finding a needle in a haystack.

The most important part to stress is that whether people find an idol or not, they all are searching, everywhere they go. High, low, under rocks, inside trees—you name it. They are searching.

When I was in Colorado, my dear friend Barb dropped some wisdom on me: "The whole world is searching. Just in the wrong places."

This isn't a new thing. In the book of Exodus, there is a prime example of searching in the wrong place.

Moses had gone to the top of Mount Sinai. While he was there, hearing from God, the Israelites down below became restless. And even though God had used Moses to lead these people out of Egypt, they still weren't satisfied and trusting that he would continue to lead them. So what did they decide? They decided they should create new gods. They melted down all the jewelry they had and created a gold calf to worship, rather than God.

Even though they had seen what God could do and that he had good plans for them, they still went searching elsewhere. The one thing that could truly bring them direction, guidance, fulfillment, and purpose was right there—and they went the other way.

You may be thinking, "Those people are crazy. I'm glad I'm not like them." However, all too often, I am reminded that we can be *exactly* like them. Now, do we melt our gold down and turn it into golden calves? Most of us, probably not. But do we have idols? Oh yeah, baby. We sure do.

An idol doesn't have to be something that we physically and tangibly bow down and worship to. As Jesus once said, "You must love the Lord your God with all your heart, all your soul, all your mind. This is the first and greatest commandment" (Matthew 22:37, NLT).

Now, I don't know about you, but there are things in my life I have loved more than God. I don't think I knew it at the moment, but there have been plenty—baseball, money, my career, future plans, working out. There have been so many seasons where my prayers were more about what these things could bring me, because those things were my idols. I prayed so heavily about them because truthfully, I wanted them more than I wanted God. The scripture above says to love God with all your heart, soul, and mind. If there is something you are loving more than God—or even evenly with God, even *close* to God—you are not, loving God with *all* your heart, soul, and mind.

"No one can serve two masters. For you will hate one and love the other; you will be devoted to one and despise the other. You cannot serve God and be enslaved to money" (Matthew 6:24, NLT).

It is God and God only. We can't choose to make God our number one and our career, spouse, passion, etc. our number one, also. You cannot serve two Gods. It is not possible, though I have tried to make it possible so many times, including on this road trip.

Like the Israelites, I had seen God guide me, deliver me, and give me purpose, but the second I lost sight of him, I began searching for idols—just like a contestant on *Survivor*.

On this trip, I idolized girls. With the amount of times people asked me if I thought I would find my wife on this trip, I began to believe I would. That seed planted made me seek *that* at times, rather than God.

I idolized the idea of relationships with Gabrielle, Grace, and Taylor throughout this trip.

Yes, I know. You're thinking that I only think about girls. And to be honest, that was absolutely true at the time. I wanted a relationship so badly. I wanted a wife. I wanted to be a husband and a father, and I still do. But at that time, I wanted it desperately. I couldn't help but think about it daily. I wanted it because I thought it was something that would "complete" me, like I wasn't already completed by Jesus Christ living in me. I wanted it because I had forgotten that my true identity was in Christ.

I saw Taylor on TikTok posting about Jesus. I direct-messaged her and we ended up FaceTiming. With the huge idol of the "idea of love" I had in my life, I always thought it would be like in the movies. I thought it would be "love at first sight," and that would be my story.

I even idolized that story. I thought there was no way I would ever meet anyone on a dating app because I couldn't tell my kids that love story. I put so much pressure into conversations with girls and set such high expectations. I wanted to make sure it would work out due to my charming personality, wittiness, and charisma. More humbly and truthfully, I wanted to control it. I didn't want to trust that God would make it happen in his timing. I didn't want to face the fact that God wanted me to just wait and submit it all to him.

Without diving too much into the Taylor story, it didn't work out. I idolized the idea of a relationship so much that when we first started FaceTiming, I couldn't function properly. When I was with my mom in Mississippi, Hannah and Kathryn in Tennessee, and everywhere in between, I was always distracted. My mind was always on the next time Taylor and I would talk, if she was the one God had for me, and so many other things. You can tell by my thoughts and actions that I was insecure. I was seeking my security and identity in a woman, not our God. Remember, you cannot serve two Gods.

I had already found my identity in Christ, but I was distracted, like a dog with a tennis ball. Like the Israelites when Moses went to the top of Mount Sinai. That's how fast it can happen. You can take your eyes off God for a minute and be sucked back into the world and your fleshly desires.

A lot of you will sit here and tell me that desiring a wife and a relationship isn't a bad thing, and I would completely agree with you. A lot of the idols in our lives may not be bad things, depending on our hearts. God has put the desire of a wife on my heart for a reason. I firmly believe that. However, he also knows my heart and its motive.

"But I, the Lord, search all hearts and examine secret motives. I give all people their due rewards, according to what their actions deserve" (Jeremiah 17:10, NLT).

My heart desired a wife for all the wrong reasons. I wanted someone to unfairly use as a source of identity and completion, for lustful desires, to not be alone, for security. I sit here thanking God that he knows my heart. If God had allowed me to pick the wrong time to find a wife, it would have been chaos and utter failure.

Today, God is changing my heart. He is teaching me to desire a woman of God to be my wife for the sake of his kingdom, so she and I together can share the Gospel, disciple those around us, and be a vessel for God's kingdom to grow. So we can complement each other, not complete each other. So we can put God first, and then each other second.

When we idolize anything, it takes us away from God and brings us closer to the world. It creates false identity and security that will never last. The other side looks like truly only serving one God—loving him with all your heart, soul, mind, and strength. It looks like *freedom*. We just have to choose it, accept it, and embrace it.

West Virginia probably would have been the best portion of the trip if I could have been truly present. My adventurous, outdoorsy, red-headed friend, Bethany, was the perfect tour guide. In our days together, we explored some of the most beautiful parts of the state. We camped out and went on amazing hikes with lookout points over miles of monstrous green trees. We enjoyed an evening at a restaurant that was right on the edge of the woods, listening to live folk music for hours on end. We explored the capital and her hometown of Marshall, sampling their finest ice cream. It was amazing, and I would have enjoyed it all that much more, if I wasn't thinking about Grace the majority of the time.

There was one segment of the trip with Bethany that I had absolutely zero thoughts of Grace. White water rafting. I had never been white water rafting, but I would go again every day of my life, if it was possible.

Bethany, me, four other strangers, and our guide rafted down New River Gorge in an inflatable boat. We raced down the river, facing extreme currents and rapids. At one point we jumped out of our boat and floated down the river, not having to put forth one ounce of effort as the current swept us along.

I learned that day that there are six classes of rapids you can face. One is very safe, and six is extremely dangerous if not handled properly. That day, we faced a class five rapid. It was the most amazing experience as the river tried to launch the boat into the sky and me with it. The rapids swirling and swirling would have no forgiveness for me—or anyone. If I were to fall out, I would have been swirled around like a sock in a washing machine until it decided to spit me back out.

With the adrenaline this experience came with and my phone left in the car, my mind was exactly where I was. I felt so free, so myself, so in awe. And although I was in a somewhat dangerous environment, I could not have felt more safe and secure.

White water rafting that day reminded me of who I am and where my identity lies: in Christ. Not in any other person, place, or thing—in Christ alone, because in Christ alone, I am free, I am myself, I am safe, I am secure. I am his.

White water rafting was such an adrenaline-filled experience that I had no choice but to be present. However, when I went streaking in Cali, I did have a choice. When Carlie and I danced outside for an hour in the middle of the rain in front of a restaurant in Kansas, we had a choice. Making these choices led to feeling free and desiring that same feeling every day of my life, if possible. And it is possible—by choosing Jesus, and only Jesus.

We have a choice. Even not choosing is a choice. We get to choose where we place our identity, in the light or in the darkness.

"Jesus spoke to the people once more and said, " I am the light of the world. If you follow me, you won't have to walk in darkness, because you will have the light that leads to life" (John 8:12, NLT).

When I think about this choice, my imagination fires up. I imagine myself in the safest place of all to me—the clouds. I imagine myself and Jesus sitting on a cloud. He's got his arm around me. When I ask him what he likes about me, he smiles, and then counts on his fingers, endlessly listing things off. Then I ask him what I do that brings him sorrow. He puts his arms out and shows me his two hands, wide open. Each hand represents a path.

One path is holding onto the world and its idols. The other is choosing Jesus and only Jesus. On his path, there is freedom, blessings, adventure, security, and a life worth living. When I choose the wrong hand, it saddens him because he knows what I am missing out on.

He wants to show me so much more. He's not angry or upset that I am not choosing him. He is saddened that I am not choosing the path that he knows is best for me.

We can choose the world and all temporary fulfillment in it. We can choose, if we want, to search and search and search for the hidden immunity idol, which will only protect you and fulfill you temporarily, or we can choose the light that leads to life. The way. The truth. The life. A daily choice. An hourly choice. A choice every second. We can choose to surrender our fleshly desires and idols, and to seek *The Spark Plug* instead. This is a choice that will give you your true identity and leave you desiring to live in it. Every. Single. Day.

So let me ask you this: What is your choice?

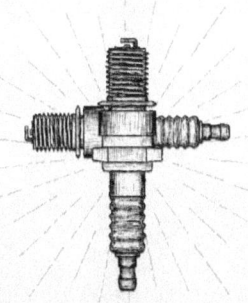

No Jumping on the Bridge

July 29 to August 5, 2021 - Tennessee
Days 64 through 71

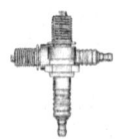

The first *hour* in Nashville, I sat in the car with my new friend, Nathan. We ate Chick-Fil-A and prayed for each other.

The first *evening* in Nashville, my new friend Emily and I met up with my old friend Dana from college for tacos. Emily and I then landed at a Nashville Sound baseball game.

The first *night* in Nashville, my other new friends, Hannah and Kathryn, took me to Krystal Burgers for what they referred to as a "life changing experience."

It's safe to say, Nashville was off to a busy start.

Day Two slowed to a more comfortable pace when Hannah, Kathryn, and myself sat down and binge watched season two of *The Outer Banks*.

After spending the whole day watching Netflix, it was time to get out of the house. We decided to hit the road for Gatlinburg, Tennessee. Our adventure in the Smoky Mountains included a roller coaster ride that glided through the mountains, cooking sizzling bacon for breakfast at our campsite, surviving the night without getting eaten by a bear, and purchasing matching sweaters to remember our trip forever. Mine was blue. The girls, yellow.

One adventure deserves its own story. This is the story of the Gatlinburg Skybridge, the longest pedestrian cable bridge in North America. It stretches almost 700 feet across a deep valley, 1,800 feet above sea level, and 500 feet above Gatlinburg. I was a little intimidated by this big bridge.

It was so high, there was a lift to get to the top. That's right—a ski lift, which felt very unsafe when we were strapped in. I use that term loosely because in fact there were no straps. Maybe it also felt unsafe because Kathryn had taken her dog, Briley, with us on this adventure. Yep—me, two women, and a grown black lab jumped onto a ski lift taking us 500 feet above the touristy town.

After purchasing a picture of us four on the lift, it was time to cross this magnificent bridge. I followed as Hannah and Kathryn took their first steps.

What was so intimidating at first was beautiful once the steps were taken. I was already in awe. Green foliage extended for miles and miles.

The bridge was super long and seemed extremely dangerous at first, but soon, I felt safe. The bridge was strong, firm, and built on a good foundation. It could carry me, Hannah, Kathryn, Briley, and at least fifty other people at the same time.

I will admit, though, I did look over the edge a few times, and that did not sit well with my stomach. Not one bit. When I took my eyes off the bridge I felt less safe.

Arriving on the other side unscathed, after a fifteen minute break, it was time to cross back over. This time around, we felt like professionals. About twenty feet before we walked over the see-through glass section, Hannah and I put our brains together and came up with an idea. Not a good one, mind you.

Hannah and I could be a little goofy and childish, while Kathryn and Briley had to play the more mature role, as the parents who can't take their kids anywhere. We proved them right when we said "Let's do a heel click!" If you aren't familiar, a heel click involves jumping up and trying to click your heels together while still in the air. It's not the easiest thing to do. It requires some practice. I recommend stretching first.

There were signs—we won't tell you we didn't see them—that said, "No jumping on the bridge," but who's to say that wasn't more of a recommendation than a requirement? Not listening to the signs, Hannah and I went for it. Three, two, one—*jump*! We did it! We even got it on video.

You know what else we got on video? An alarm sounding, followed by a man yelling through a megaphone, "No jumping on the bridge!"

Whoops. In retrospect, it wasn't very smart, but this chapter wouldn't exist otherwise. God knew what he was doing.

When Hannah and I jumped, that was scary. I did not feel one ounce of safety in my body. Upon landing, I swear I felt the bridge sway more than it already was, left to right like a pendulum. After getting yelled at, I have to admit some embarrassment and shame. All the people around us were probably thinking how stupid we were.

So, hear me out. The bridge is God. The bridge is strong, sturdy, and when followed—unwavering. The bridge lays out a clear path— the bridge *is* the path. Stay on it, keep your eyes on it, and remain safe. When on the bridge, you experience all the beauty around you, the awe of the bridge and the places it can bring you.

The bridge is also Jesus.

"Jesus spoke to the people once more and said, " I am the light of the world. If you follow me, you won't have to walk in darkness, because you will have the light that leads to life" (John 8:12, NLT).

In the last chapter, we discussed a choice. The right choice is right above: the choice to follow Jesus, to walk with him, as he is the light that leads to life. The choice is to let *The Spark Plug* ignite your life.

Just like with following Jesus, we had a choice on the bridge. We could follow the path, or we could stray away from the path. What happened when we strayed away?

1) I took my eyes off of the safety of the path, looked down, and felt frightened and unsafe.
2) Hannah and I jumped on the bridge, not following the guidelines of the path, and we suffered the consequences, including shame.

Not choosing Jesus is choosing the alternative. The alternative of the light is darkness. Darkness keeps your eyes off the bridge, bringing fear, shame, insecurity, depression, anxiety, feelings of being lost and stuck, and so much more. When you try to look anywhere other than the path of Jesus, you will inevitably feel like you are being swung back and forth, left to right, like a pendulum.

To follow Jesus is a long path. Although it may feel winding and dangerous sometimes, keeping your eyes on him will get you where you need to be, in safety. Jesus is our solid foundation. He is strong, sturdy, and more than capable of bearing all of our burdens.

A relationship with him may seem intimidating at first. It sometimes may even seem like the "boring" path. And because we are humans, we may turn our heads away from the signs every once in a while. We may even jump off the path, yet he still wants us and loves us. He still catches us and desires for us to return to the straight path of awe and beauty, the path of pursuing him.

He just wants you to seek the light. There is never so much darkness in your life that you cannot access the light. The light is everywhere. Darkness is nowhere. Darkness is the absence of light—that is it. Light *always* overpowers darkness! So if you are feeling in the dark, like you're swaying back and forth, looking in the wrong places, I urge you: flip the switch and turn on the light. He will catch you and still welcome you on his strong, beautiful bridge, any day of the week.

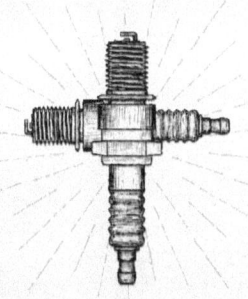

THE SAVANNAH BANANAS

August 5 to August 7, 2021 - Georgia
Days 71 through 73

I f you don't know who the Savannah Bananas are, you may live under a technological rock, oblivious to social media. I don't intend for this to upset you. I am simply saying if you have not heard of them, there is absolutely no way you are consistently active on social media, because they are *viral times viral times viral.* And I am jealous of your simplistic lifestyle.

If you are part of the small percentage of people who have never heard of the Bananas, let me enlighten you. The Savannah Bananas have brought "America's Pastime," baseball, back to life. One could say the Bananas are the "Harlem Globetrotters" of baseball. They are no ordinary team.

What's so different about this baseball team? One word: everything.

1) They are called the Bananas.
2) They do any and every kind of trick play. Players will catch a ball as they are in the middle of a front flip.
3) They have a player named "stilts," who of course walks around wearing stilts, towering many feet above the other players.
4) Dancing. Yep. Coaches dance. Players dance. Umpires dance, shaking their booties for the crowd.
5) Players go into the crowd. They may do a multitude of things such as singing to fans, handing out roses to pretty

girls, dancing on top of the dugouts, holding a baby to the sky as music from Lion King plays.

6) If a fan catches a foul ball, the batter is out. This is part of their "Banana ball" rules.

7) Somewhere in the mix of all of that, they play baseball.

The list is limitless. The Savannah Bananas are pure entertainment. You could take any person in the world to a game, and they would have a hard time telling you they were bored. Baseball has a reputation of being boring by many, but the Savannah Bananas are anything but boring.

After Nashville, I drove down to Savannah, Georgia. The only thing I was prepared for was the trees. One of my best friends, who had previously spent a summer in Georgia, told me, "Dude, look at the trees. They're like Harry Potter trees." I didn't really understand until I was there myself.

Walking through historic, downtown Savannah, I experienced the huge, mossy, "Harry Potter" trees. Beautiful Savannah was one part of the trip I had the pleasure of doing alone. I did not find any Georganites to host me and due to that, I had a free Friday evening. What better way than to spend it at a Savannah Bananas playoff game?

The Savannah Bananas experience was like nothing else, starting with the food. I was given a meal ticket in the beginning and told I could use it for unlimited burgers, hot dogs, chips, and drinks. That's right, *unlimited*. I went back for "seconds" and felt like I was robbing the place when I was handed a cheeseburger and bag of chips, for a second time, without additional payment. That was enough to make me happy, and it only got better.

There was a band that trotted through the stadium playing "Hey Baby" by Bruce Channel or DJ Otzi. In fact, if you haven't heard this song, turn it on right now for the experience. Both versions.

The players were dancing among the crowd, spinning their shirts above their heads.

The announcer walked through the stands and talked to fans during the game. The energy in the stadium was unmatchable. Trying to look around and find someone not smiling, laughing, or enjoying themselves was harder than a game of *Where's Waldo?* The vibes were so contagious that I had an urge of confidence to tap the three fans in front of me on the shoulders and ask if I could join them for the game. It was a blast, and everyone left way happier than when they walked in.

That's the story of the Savannah Bananas playoff game.

Wait!

Aren't I missing an important piece of information? The score? Who won? That's right. The Bananas lost. They lost game two of a three-game series. If they would have won, they would have been champions of the league. Since they lost, they were forced to play game three, a winner takes all game, the next evening.

Guess what? Nobody cared. Nobody cared about the result of the Bananas losing. Would it have been cool to see the Bananas dogpile? Absolutely—but it wasn't about the result.

I know this may be hard to comprehend for some of you. I used to be an athlete. I used to coach. Winning was so important. Winning was the source of stress. We had to earn the victory and if we didn't, falling short was painful. If we lost, we weren't good enough. We had to get better. This message is pushed too hard in athletics today, from youth to professionals—and I was part of that problem, at times, when I coached.

The obsession with victory taught me that I had to earn my coach telling me "good job" and "I'm proud of you." It taught me that I wasn't good enough if I wasn't the winner. And due to that, I desired to win so badly. My teams did win, a lot. It was fun, but when we lost—it wasn't fun. My self-worth and value were dependent on my performance.

Sadly, this hasn't always just applied to sports. Someone told me recently that how you have viewed love in your life is sometimes how you view God's love. That's when I realized, throughout multiple relationships in my life, I have sought love via my performance. I thought I had to earn it. I had to do enough, be enough, give enough. I thought I had to do the right things. I even started to picture God's love for me that way. And The Savannah Bananas taught me one thing: none of this is true.

The true model for love is *The Spark Plug*. The model for love is Jesus. He loves us so much. He came down from heaven into our world to save and redeem us. To set us free. To give us an eternity with our creator. Jesus lived a life faced with temptation, mockery, and hatred toward him. He was spit on, stripped of his clothing, brutally flogged, and nailed to a cross. He was crucified for us, while we were still sinners. He doesn't just forgive us of our sins, but he forgets our sins. To him, we are washed white as snow. We are perfect. All he wants is our hearts. If we turn away, he accepts us back with open arms, no matter what we have done. No matter how far away we are. Jesus is the true model for unconditional love.

Since we already have his love, we can't *earn* his love, so do not fall into the trap of believing you have to earn it, that you are not "doing enough." Faith isn't about earning the love of our father. If we had to earn his love, that would take away from the love and the relationship. God wants our hearts, not our performance. What Jesus did on the cross is all about love and relationship.

He died so we could know how much he loved us, and so we could spend our time in heaven and on earth with him. There is nothing we can do to make him love us more or less. Nothing can separate us from God's love. His love is so unfathomable, and it will be until the day we die. It is the purest, most amazing, most perfect love available. All we have to do is accept it.

There is one true love. It stems from Jesus. Jesus is your biggest fan. He sits in the front row every single day, cheering you on. He is an audience of one. He loves being in your presence, no matter what. He loves every single thing about you. He is always joyfully watching you. And even when you feel like you are not good enough, he is dancing with joy and eating unlimited hot dogs, grinning, because he loves you no matter what.

You don't earn this father's love. You sit in it. You accept it. Because there is nothing you can do, no result you can construct, that will change how much his heart longs for and loves you. That is the perfect, real, endless, amazing love of *The Spark Plug*. When you truly know and accept this love, how can you not go forth and share it, and share it, and share it, making it viral times viral times viral?

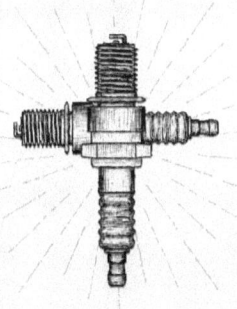

TIMING

August 8 to August 14, 2021 - South Dakota
Days 74 through 80

T iming is everything. The world is nonstop, continuously spinning, and yet, everything is timed so perfectly. Like the night my dad walked into a bar in New York and met my mom, ultimately leading to my existence. Like the release of a basketball out of a player's hands a split second before the clock expires. Like a parachute opening as a skydiver is plummeting toward the Earth. It can be a matter of meeting your future spouse, winning or losing the big game, or even life and death. Timing is everything. And sure enough, our perfect God is perfect in his timing.

At the halfway point, twenty-four states in, when people backed out on me in Florida and South Carolina, God's perfect timing showed.

From May 27th to August 10th, this was my schedule: drive from one state to another (this would take anywhere from two to ten hours), spend anywhere from one to seven days in that state, meet at least one new person in every state, get to know the new person by telling them all about myself and getting to know more about them, explore and adventure their state with them nonstop with minimal to no rest, say goodbye, then do it all over again. This was an amazing trip. This was the most amazing experience of my life, but man, it was so exhausting. By the time I was twenty-four states and two and a half months in, I needed a break. I was burned out and needed new life.

After the Savannah Bananas game, I went straight to my motel and booked a flight home for a week. While having people back out on me had caused worry before, I now saw it as a blessing and was able to take advantage.

I was so ready to be home. I wanted to be with my family and friends. I wanted to be in my community that God had blessed me with. I wanted to sleep. In reality, I was ready to quit.

It was at this point that I had truly learned quitting is okay. I had the revelation that if you are fully content in moving in a new direction in your life, at peace with it, and it is in line with God's will, it is completely okay. No more of this toxic, worldly belief that you must finish everything you start, even if it is harmful and unhealthy to you.

That wasn't my circumstance, though. My circumstance was that I desired to quit because I was tired and it was hard—but God had created this trip and meant for me to finish it with him. I am so glad that I walked in line with his plan, rather than my own.

As mentioned, his timing is so perfect that when you feel like you can't breathe and you are sinking deep into the depths of the dark ocean, he lifts you up for the best breath of fresh air you could experience.

My breath of fresh air came the second I walked out of the airport. I was surprisingly greeted by my sister, niece, and nephew. I was expecting only my mom. Driving back home with those I loved was bittersweet. I felt as though my niece and nephew had doubled in age and size in just two months.

If I simply had lunch with them and went straight back to Florida, I would have been one of the most content men on earth—but *The Spark Plug* had plans.

That week, I had lunch with my dad, spent time on the lake with family, caught up with friends, dove into my community, and received encouragement from everyone. But there was one moment that made the week.

Tanner.

Wanting to milk every second I had of being back home, my friends and I were being hoodlums—as much as you can be, as sober Christians late at night. We were walking downtown, singing and dancing, knocking out sets of push-ups. We stopped at a random sidewalk in downtown Sioux Falls, laid ourselves down, and stared into the night sky, content. Just being still and being in each other's presence, enjoying life.

It had to have been at least 11 p.m., if not later, when a random dude on this warm August night came RipStiking (a RipStik is basically a cooler, newer, skateboard) meticulously around our bodies to avoid hitting us.

One of my friends called out to the ripsticker, "Tanner?"

Tanner hopped off his board and started to chat it up with this guy. There was something about Tanner that was extremely appealing—I think it was that he was super genuine and kind. He went around introducing himself to everyone in a calm manner, then conversed with every one of us.

After interviewing everyone, I was up. I told Tanner a little bit about myself—and how could I not mention the forty-eight-state road trip I was in the middle of? Tanner not only loved what God was doing, but there was something about our conversation that was unlike ones I had been having in recent states. It was relaxing, calming, and life giving.

Before we knew it, Tanner was a part of our group for the night. The hoodlumness continued. Being two blocks behind my home church, which conveniently has an apartment with a pool in its backyard, someone very excitedly suggested "We should jump in the pool!" It was a split vote. Half excited, half hesitant.

Tanner looked at me and said, "I trust this guy. I'm doing what Stephen does."

And so he did what I did.

Feeling like I had just met a new brother, feeling full of life, I went down to my core mantras: live life to the fullest, risk it to get the biscuit, through God for God, weird and awkward. The decision was simple.

We hopped the fence and plunged ourselves into the body of water. The fearlessness was contagious. Tanner and I were the first in the pool, then two more, then everyone. Splashing around in this pool we clearly were not supposed to be in filled me with adrenaline and excitement.

Now, I'm not saying to go ahead and live life as a rule breaker, but I am saying if you are ever faced with an opportunity to live life fully and you know, deep in your gut, it will be awesome and not hurt anyone, do the dang thing. If God can work in everything, he most certainly can work in that.

Tanner, soaked from head to toe, requested a ride home. I was glad to take Tanner home and drop him off. A five-minute drive home turned into an hour-long conversation. You could feel God in the middle. How do I know? Because anything *The Spark Plug* is in the center of has more life. The conversation ranged from girls and love to God and faith to promising we would invite each other to our weddings. It ended with a bro hug and an, "I love you, bro." I've only ever told a couple dudes I love them upon our first meeting. The commonality? God was in the center.

Years later, Tanner and I are still good buddies. We both know God more than we did then. We both happen to be writing books.

And every time I see him, I am blessed with that calm demeanor and reminded of God's timing in everything.

If I hadn't gone home that week, I probably would have quit the trip, limiting God's plans. If I wasn't lying on a sidewalk at 11 p.m. and Tanner wasn't RipStiking by, I would have never gotten that encouragement, life, and a new brother in Christ.

Timing is everything. The world is nonstop, continuously spinning, and yet, everything is timed so perfectly. Like when people left me homeless for a week in the southeast United States, so I had to fly home. Like the time I met Tanner and his RipStik on the sidewalk. Like the time we jumped into the pool. It can be a matter of hope or hopelessness, giving up or trekking on, meeting an amazing person, or being filled with life. Timing is everything. And sure enough, our perfect God is perfect in his timing.

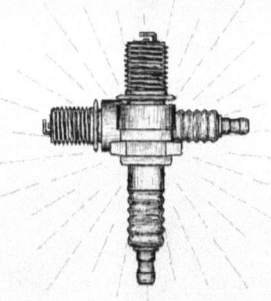

WHO YOU KNOW

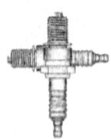

"It's not about what you know, it's about who you know."
They drilled this one-liner into our brains in college,
always stressing that the connections we make will lead to
real opportunities. As I grow older, I find this to be truer than I
believed it to be then.

Two years ago, I secured a job coaching college softball. This job
was offered to me by an old friend who I went to graduate school
with. Now, I was familiar with coaching, but only baseball. I had
never coached a day of softball in my life. I knew nothing about it.

The next job was managing a convenience store. I knew
absolutely nothing about gas stations. For about two months my
employees knew more about the job than I did. Maybe that's why
half of them quit right away.

"It's not about what you know, it's about who you know" rings
true in my life. Recently, I've realized there is an even deeper meaning.

My good friend and I were talking about God and being in
relation with him. He said the all too common line: "I don't know
enough." He meant that he didn't know enough about God to
share him with others. He felt he had to have a certain amount of
knowledge to do it right.

I didn't realize it at the time, but it was the Holy Spirit that gave
me a very profound statement for my friend: "It's not about what
you know. It's about who you know."

My friend has a personal relationship with Jesus. Jesus has done things in my friends life and is continuing to write an amazing testimony. My friend knows the truth of Jesus and has accepted it! What else does he have to know? Nothing!

When I started at the gas station, *I knew absolutely nothing* about the job. But today, over a year into the position, I can manage the store in fifteen hours per week, allowing me time to write a book. I didn't know anything about the job at first, but *I kept showing up.* The whole time I leaned on the one I knew, my mother (also boss). Now, I am very confident in many things in the industry, more than I ever anticipated I would be.

My relationship with Jesus is parallel. I hopped into the baptismal tank with honestly very little understanding or knowledge of what I was doing, or even about Christ. I just had a sensational feeling that I needed to get baptized that day. Over the last four years, I have done nothing but continue to show up in my relationship with God. The whole time I leaned on the one that I knew, Jesus. I grew to know him more, and with that, I grew to "know more." And I do feel more "equipped" to go and share Jesus with others, now. I feel more equipped, but I don't know if that makes it easier.

When I first gave my life to Christ, there was a heart change. There was transformation. I had this strong desire to go and tell people and show them what God had done and what he was doing. The point being, I didn't really know anything. I just knew Jesus and that he had changed my life, and I had to tell others. I kind of wish sometimes I was still in that stage of life, because I occasionally forget how much Christ has changed me. I know a lot more about him now, but if I am not careful, I can easily seek learning more *about* Jesus than actually *seeking Jesus.* So let me tell you some stories.

MACK AND MADDIE

I had the pleasure of knowing Mack and Maddie before my trip began. I had coached Mack a few years prior, while he was playing college baseball. I met Maddie at a bar in Nashville, TN and we hit it off.

Regardless of the origin stories, I was blessed to know two people who lived on the east side of the country. Mack was in Asheville, North Carolina and Maddie was in the Northeast—she lived in Connecticut, but she and I ventured to Rhode Island and I helped her move to Boston. I assisted in packing, followed her dad, Harry, in the U-Haul, helped put together the bed, organized the closet, and hung the lights and frames on the wall. Yes, I am available for hire.

August 14 to August 17, 2021 - North Carolina
Days 80 through 83

Anyway, I was very fortunate to stay with Mack in North Carolina. He was excited to host me as we scraped our plans together over Snapchat messages. It was great to hang out with someone familiar. The pressure was also lessened on his end—unlike my other hosts, he didn't have to host a random stranger. His point of view was, "Ozzy" (my coaching name) is coming to stay and hang out for a couple nights, and we will explore a bit together. All pressure was off on both ends. We could just chill and hang out.

Besides going out to eat, checking out some downtown breweries, and watching movies, there were two main memories that I stored away from my time with him. 1) Running around Mack's apartment complex in the pouring rain for a mile. 2) Going for a hike through the gorgeous Blue Ridge Mountains.

The run is pretty self-explanatory and I probably don't need to dive into any more details, other than that it was awesome. But let's talk more about the Mountains. I had never heard of the Blue Ridge Mountains prior to staying with Mack. Honestly, if I hadn't visited Mack, there's a good chance I still wouldn't have heard of them.

It was a gloomy, foggy hike. When we reached the top lookout point where we were supposed to see mountains for miles and miles, all we saw was white, hazy, clouds. Mack was disappointed. I was in awe of the beauty and taking in something I would never forget. Although I didn't see the mountains on the horizon, it was still an amazing experience I would not trade away.

It could very well be a matter of expectations and perspective. Mack had seen the view before, without clouds. He knew how amazing it was. I had never been there before. I had never even heard of these mountains.

It wasn't what I knew that got me into this situation—I knew nothing about North Carolina. I didn't know what mountains were or weren't there. I didn't even know what I was supposed to see past the clouds.

I knew Mack. Mack gave me a place to stay. Mack gave me comfort and companionship. Mack brought me to a place I never would have brought myself if I didn't have his guidance. It's not about what you know (or don't know). It's about who you know.

August 31 to September 4, 2021 - Connecticut, Rhode Island, Massachusetts
Days 97 through 101

Although I lived in New York for the first five years of my life, believe it or not, I knew very little about the Northeast. Luckily, I knew a nice girl named Maddie. The night I met Maddie in Nashville has no other explanation than it being miraculous timing. I was visiting Nashville for a conference and she was there with her friends on a weekend trip. We met at a bar, had a great time, and

I said if I ever were to go to Boston, where she was in school, I would visit.

We talked a lot about the song "Boston" by Augustana. Then I proceeded to Snapchat while singing to her the next couple years every time that song came on. Sidenote: singing a song in the city it is about is one of the most exhilarating things you can do—"Boston" in Boston, "Paint me a Birmingham" in Birmingham, etc. You have to try it sometime.

Back to the story. I never thought Maddie and I would actually meet again. It never really connected in my head until I was about five miles from her parents' house in Connecticut. It got real when I was riding shotgun with her, driving around her hometown, letting my hand glide through the wind outside the window like a surfer catching waves.

Like in North Carolina, I had very little expectations as far as what lay ahead. I just had high expectations of the person I was going to be staying with. I knew Maddie was awesome. I didn't know much at all about Connecticut, Rhode Island, or Massachusetts. I did know the Red Sox played in Boston—that's about it. Lucky for me, I didn't have to know a lot. I just had to know one person.

Like with Mack, Maddie was under less pressure. She knew me. We had only met once, but it was one of those friendships where you just vibe. Right away, you know the other person is cool and you connect. Maybe that's Maddie with everyone. I wouldn't doubt it, because she is just so authentically herself. Either way, she wanted to show me the awesome states around her, but she didn't have some long list of things we had to do. She simply invited me into her life for a couple days and let me join in.

In Connecticut, that meant meeting one of her friends for a few drinks, making her parents dinner, watching a movie, and playing some ping pong. Yes, I lost.

In Rhode Island, it meant exploring Watch Hill, a town alongside the ocean. The Watch Hill experience included driving by a house that Taylor Swift apparently used to live in, trying new seafood, and diving into the rushing ocean.

For it being September 1st, it was not your typical beach day, but it was one of those moments when you recognize and appreciate what is in front of you. What was in front of me was maybe one of my last opportunities for a while that I'd have to strip down to my banana-print boxers and jump into the Atlantic Ocean. So, that is exactly what we did—took advantage of the opportunity in front of us. That chilly September day, Maddie and I made a memory. Lesson from Watch Hill: always jump in the ocean.

Connecticut and Rhode Island point only one way: Boston. Or as the native folk pronounce it, Bah-stin. Boston is where the magic happened. After successfully moving Maddie into her new place and meeting her new roommates all within the span of six hours, we got down to business. We joined her sister and brother-in-law for their co-ed softball game.

Maddie knew I loved baseball. If anyone else was hosting a stranger in their city, their first thought probably wouldn't be, "I should take him to play softball with my family!" But Maddie knew me. And so, we played softball.

My first at-bat, the first pitch was high and in. I turned my hands inside the ball and smacked it, launching the ball. Foul ball. Next pitch. If the pitcher would have learned, he would have known not to throw another high one. With the pitch at chest height, I took a wack and watched the ball leave the sight of my bat, flying high and far over the left fielder's head. Now, if we had fences, it's probably a home run. This park had character though—it had no fence in left field, and the right field fence was trees. Without a barrier to signify a home run or not, I dodged out of the box knowing without a doubt that I was going to touch all four bases and get an inside-the-park home run. Having rained the night before, the field was quite muddy. While taking a wide turn around first base, I lost my feet in the muck and fell right on my butt.

Laughing hysterically, I got up and completed my swift run around the bases, still getting a home run. This is when I felt that God had wanted to tell me, "You might fall while going around the bases, Stephen. But I will always pick you up and get you home."

That was a magical moment. And so were the next days with Maddie. Since we knew each other well enough, it was easier to have real conversations. That includes real conversations about *The Spark Plug*.

I'll never forget one comment Maddie made about our God conversations. At one point, while walking to a Red Sox game, she said, "I really like your faith." The cool thing is that my faith is no different than a faith Maddie or anyone else can have. No different than a faith you can have. My faith is in Jesus. The way, the truth, the life.

"I am the way, the truth, and the life. No one can come to the father except through me" (John 14:6, NLT).

A lot of people don't like this message because they think this message is exclusive. It is. It is exclusive in the fact that truly there is only one way. Jesus. He is the only way. But, on the other end, it is also the most inclusive truth you will hear in your whole entire life. Jesus is the only way, but Jesus is for everyone. Everyone. Not one specific group of people—the whole entire world. Jesus is for every single person.

I believe that is what Maddie loved about "my faith." She liked that it could be for her. It can be for Maddie, me, and you. It can be for everyone.

Boston with Maddie was perfect. Maddie and I went for a four-mile run though town and rode Blue Bikes near Harvard University. We walked the Freedom Trail. Maddie introduced me to Acai bowls and helped me knock something off of my lifetime bucket list: going to a Boston Red Sox game. As Maddie and I sang "Sweet Caroline" during the seventh-inning stretch, I couldn't help but think how glad I was to know Maddie.

If I didn't know Maddie, I would never have had a personal tour of Watch Hill, played softball in Boston, or had any of the amazing conversations and experiences that I had in the Northeast. Without knowing Maddie, it would have been a whole different story. And let me remind you, it is the same with Jesus. It's not about what you know. It's about who you know.

THE EAST COAST

August 20 to August 23, 2021 - Kentucky,
Virginia, Maryland, Delaware
Days 86 through 89

Mack and Maddie exhibit how not knowing much about something, but knowing the right person, can help you learn more than you could ever imagine. They set the example that you don't have to know a lot, you just have to get to know Jesus. Knowing him and following him will give you the way, the truth, and the life. He will give you guidance, direction, knowledge, life changes, and so much more.

But what if you don't know a lot about something, *and* you don't know a person? Meaning, what if you don't know a lot *about* Jesus, but you also don't *know* Jesus?

After I left West Virginia, I had two days to travel and explore Kentucky, Virginia, Maryland, and Delaware. You may ask, why so fast? Well, at the halfway point, when God timed out my break perfectly, I recalibrated. I decided I would still go to every state where someone had backed out on me, but instead of searching frantically for people to help me at the last second, I would just visit the state briefly on my own, and be on my way.

I left West Virginia with one goal in mind: find stickers, shot glasses, and postcards in these states. I had been collecting these in every single state and would not move on until I had them all. I collected a sticker for my water bottle, a sticker for my car door, a postcard to write down memories and lessons from the trip, and a shot glass that I may never drink out of.

In Kentucky, it was very hard to find a gift shop with the items I was looking for. Since I couldn't find any information online, I just drove west. I got off multiple exits and searched for anything I could find. With no luck, I finally found Grayson, Kentucky—a very small town, but I was optimistic. I stopped at three department stores, all stocked with zilch, squat, nada.

I tried one more spot downtown that I was certain would not have what I needed. Surprisingly, they did. In small-town Grayson, I was able to find my souvenirs in a downtown sports store.

After scouring Kentucky to find my souvenirs, I turned right around and headed straight to Virginia, where I planned to stay the night. Like Kentucky, I knew no one in Virginia, so the only plan I had was to find my treasures and sleep.

Google led me to an amazing lookout point, and my meager knowledge of Virginia led me to drive by Virginia Commonwealth University. Both of these things sound amazing, but they weren't. I didn't know about the lookout point, so I didn't get there in time for most of the sunset. If I would have been aware of it sooner or knew someone who knew to take me there, I would have experienced more than a three-minute sunset. Although still beautiful, it could have been so much better. As for visiting VCU, I literally just drove by the campus. And the same thing happened the next day, in Maryland—I visited the University of Maryland because I knew for sure I would find souvenirs there. I was able to walk around the campus, but without knowing anyone there to actually show me around or give me access to the buildings, I was lost.

And that's the whole point. I didn't know much about Kentucky, Virginia, or Maryland at all. I didn't know anyone in those states, either. Because of that, I drove through many counties and visited many stores aimlessly. I missed the sunset in Virginia, because I wasn't from around there and didn't know until last minute there was a beautiful lookout over the city. I knew a little bit about the two colleges, but I didn't know anyone there.

Not knowing a lot *about* Jesus is okay, because we all start there—but not *knowing* Jesus is where you become lost. Jesus is our path, compass, light, way—however you want to say it, knowing Jesus is the most important thing in life. Without knowing him, you are disconnected from the true source of life.

> Yes, I am the vine; you are the branches. Those who remain in me, and I in them will produce much fruit. For apart from me you can do nothing. Anyone who does not remain in me is thrown away like a useless branch and withers. (John 15:5-6a, NLT)

Jesus is the vine and we are the branches, but when we choose to not follow him and get to know him, we are branches removed from the source of life; lifeless. We are lost.

If I would have known people in those states like Mack and Maddie, I know my experiences would have been completely

STEPHEN JOHN OSWALD JR

different. And God works all things for our good. He still allowed me to see a beautiful sunset and enjoy some alone time, and he gave me a story to tell. I just can't help but think about what those states could have been like if I had known someone in them.

Like I said, It's not about what we know. It's about who we know. Even if you don't know Jesus, he wants you more than anything. He doesn't want you to be lifeless and lost. He wants you to be found. Found in him, and full of life.

DEVIN

September 16 to September 21 - Indiana
Days 113 through 118

Let's review some combinations of knowing. There is not knowing a lot about Jesus, *but* knowing Jesus. There is not knowing a lot about Jesus, *and not* knowing Jesus. What else could there be? One more thought comes to mind. Knowing a lot about Jesus, but *choosing not* to personally know and follow Jesus. In other words, knowing all about Jesus, but choosing to not be in relationship with him.

I went to college in Indianapolis, IN. In those four years, I explored, adventured, and experienced the state of Indiana—it's fair to say that I became knowledgeable and comfortable with the area. Comfortable enough that if I was passing through the state on my own, I could find somewhere to stay and fun things to do. I know the state of Indiana.

Devin and I met in our sophomore year of college. We had in common the fact that we had each quit our respective college sports. I hung up the cleats and he hung up the goggles. We instantly connected and became best friends. Our desire to live life fully and be ourselves while doing it blossomed into a beautiful friendship.

To this day, every time we hang out, we make sure to jam-pack our time with adventures and great memories. A summer before this amazing road trip, I called Devin and asked if he would host me in Indy for a couple days. When you think about visiting an old friend on a trip, I am sure you get very excited about spending time with each other and adventuring, but I assure you, nothing you have experienced compares to Devin and me reconnecting. Nothing.

I'd only notified Devin less than a week in advance that I would visit him, so we really didn't have time to make plans. I just knew I wanted to see one of my best friends and go skydiving.

Devin and I spent three days together. Here is what we did: drove to Nashville after he got off work; played at a casino in Kentucky until around 2 a.m.; continued to Nashville; took a thirty-minute nap at our hotel; hopped on a bus that took us to Lynchburg, TN for a Jack Daniel's distillery tour; rode back to Nashville; immediately went on a helicopter ride; took another short nap; went out in downtown Nashville and stayed at the house of someone we met; woke up and threw up early in the morning with a hangover—remember, God has changed me a lot; drove the whole day back to Indiana to go skydiving; headed back to Indy to see our other good friend Marty and go swimming; and finally, enjoyed another casino that night with our friend Jason. I think we may have snuck a trip to the movie theatre in there, too. I think that's it. Like I said, Devin and I are all about adventure and living life to the fullest.

Indiana was actually the very last state of my road trip—the forty-eighth and final state. I knew there was only one way to go out: with a bang, and what better way to go out than to end the trip with Devin?

This time around, Devin and I followed suit and crushed our time together, yet again. This is what we accomplished: attended a drive-in movie while eating Raisin Bran and healthy snacks from Target; called EMS to help a woman that had fainted right in front of us on Eagle Creek Trail; separated a fight in line at the casino because of "cutting"; talked about God and attended church; Go Karted and Top Golfed; got in sensory deprivation tanks; saw another movie; and admittedly hit the casino again with Marty and Devin (God is always refining). We may not have been thousands of miles into the sky this time around, but we sure took advantage of our limited time together.

I knew a whole lot about Indiana prior to both of these trips. I very easily could have stayed in Indiana by myself and relied on my knowledge to know which sights to see and which places to explore.

But it's not about what you know. It's about who you know. And I know Devin. Devin is one of my best friends who is and always will be there for me. Every time I go to Indy, I will always reach out to Devin. Marty, too. No matter how much I know about Indiana, I will always connect with Devin and Marty, because I have a *relationship* with these guys. I know them and they know me. We love each other. We are always there for each other. When I visit them, what I know about the state of Indiana doesn't matter. We could sit on a couch for three days straight and not step outside the house once, and it would be a successful trip to Indiana. Because it's all about who I know, not what I know.

The same goes with Jesus. I could read the Bible front to back countless times. I could study every aspect of his life. I could know everything about the church and religion. I could know everything about Jesus. But unless I actually *know* Jesus, really know him with all my heart, it doesn't matter how much I know.

If you openly declare that Jesus is Lord and believe in your heart that God raised him from the dead, you will be saved. For it is by believing in your heart that you are made right with God, and it is by openly declaring your faith that you are saved. (Romans 10:9-10, NLT)

Take that scripture in. Nowhere does it say, "by openly declaring your knowledge of God in your head." It's not about the head knowledge. It's about the heart transformation. It's not about the routines of faith. It's about the relationship with your father. A relationship with God is easy. A relationship with God looks like a relationship with Devin. Spending time with him, being with him, talking with him, being in his presence, being open to going wherever he takes you, being loved by him, and loving him back.

It's not about what you know. It's about who you know. I think it's time we start drilling that into everyone's hearts right now. If you don't know enough, that's okay. Jesus just wants you to know him. If you don't know Jesus, that's okay. He just wants you to get to know him. If you know everything there is to know about Jesus, but don't know him personally, that's okay. He's patiently waiting for you. He just wants your heart. He just wants you. Remember, it's never been about what you know. It will always be about who you know. It will always be about *The Spark Plug*.

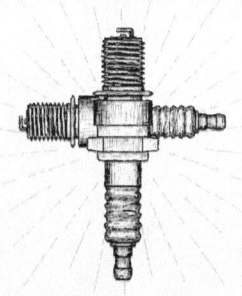

WAIT

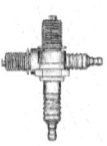

"Jesus was about thirty years old when he began his public ministry" (Luke 3:23, NLT).

"Once when he was done eating with them, he commanded them, 'Do not leave Jerusalem until the Father sends you the gift he promised, as I told you before. John baptized with water, but in just a few days you will be baptized with the Holy Spirit'" (Acts 1:4-5, NLT).

"Crowds of sick people- blind, lame, or paralyzed- lay on the porches. One of the men lying there had been waiting thirty-eight years. When Jesus saw him and knew he had been ill for a long time, he asked him, 'Would you like to get well?'" (John 5:3-6, NLT).

I could go on and on, but I think you get the point. *Waiting is inevitable.* Jesus waited thirty years to start his ministry. The disciples waited for the Holy Spirit to fall on them before they went forward sharing Jesus. The man at the pool of Bethesda waited thirty-eight years before he could walk.

Are you waiting for something in your life from God? Me too. And I feel like I have been for a while. The man at the pool of Bethesda has given me a little perspective in my season of waiting, but no matter what, waiting is still waiting. Waiting is hard, but the lessons to be learned can be invaluable and life changing.

NEW JERSEY

August 23 to August 25, 2021 - New Jersey
Days 89 through 91

You know what sounds really good right now? Buffalo Wild Wings. Like, really good.

It also sounded really good to Jill, Gabby, and me after we spent hours jumping at an indoor trampoline park with all the kids in Parsippany, NJ. Looking to satisfy our hunger, we sat down ready to indulge in some of America's finest wings.

This was the first day I had met Jill and Gabby. Conversation was not dry, as it is very easy for me to talk with strangers about the last twenty-five years of my life. I'd say there was a lot of "catching up" to be done. So, when we realized the conversion started to dry up after an hour, that prompted the question, "Where is our food?"

Now, I am a huge "bdubs" fan. I will always be in their corner, but after waiting for two hours for our very simple order, my new friends and I were getting a little tired of waiting. We finally arrived at the discussion of whether we should leave or not.

I, myself, really wanted to stay, because how much longer could it be? We had already been waiting two hours. But burning off calories at the trampoline complex had me irrationally hungry. My logic was that if we left, it would take us even longer to get food. We would have to leave, find a new place to eat, order, and then who knows how long we would have to wait for that food. We were near to being impatient and going down a different path—even though we were so close to our wings. I suggested that I go pee and if the food wasn't at our table by the time I arrived back, we could go somewhere else.

It's a good thing I drank a lot of water in those two hours. It's also good that I intentionally took extra time washing my hands and fixing my hair. As I walked back to the table, I saw the most majestic sight a hungry man could see: a huge platter full of boneless, honey barbecue wings, fried pickles, and—of course—overflowing cups of ranch. The timing was perfect, and I could not have been more grateful. We stayed, enjoyed our meal, and were on our way.

Comparing the wait for wings to waiting on God seems silly, but the shoe fits. As we've mentioned, his timing is always perfect. But that's not all. There is so much gratitude and fulfillment to be found in the waiting. Although it was hard to wait for that food, it tasted way better than if it was served right away, because I craved it that much more. I learned to appreciate it more because I had to suffer a little bit along the way.

You may be extremely close to whatever you are waiting for, so stay patient and obedient. If we had left five minutes sooner, we never would have received our food. If we decided to choose a different path, we never would have reaped the reward, and the same goes for God. I know you may be tired of waiting, but stay patient wherever he has you. *The Spark Plug* is already cooking something up. And it smells really good.

WHALE WAITING

August 25 to August 28, 2021 - New York
Days 91 through 94

After waiting for some tasty wings in New Jersey, getting a Cross tattoo on my left wrist, and having a sparkler party at Asbury Park Beach, the journey continued. Linnea from Long Island, New York was next on the docket.

One amazing thing about meeting strangers all across the country is being reminded of how uniquely made every single person is. God has created us all to be unique. I met so many people with completely different beliefs, lifestyles, and passions. I loved Linnea's passion—not only her passion for Christ, but for the ocean, and specifically what is in the ocean.

Linnea took me to an aquarium on our last day together. You might think that would be my only aquatic experience of the trip— *au contraire*. Not only did I go to an aquarium, but I also went on a boat that went miles and miles out onto the Atlantic Ocean to try to capture the beautiful visual of a whale. Oh yeah, did I mention Linnea was the tour guide?

Yep. Linnea's job was to hop on a huge boat—let's just call it a ship, because "boat" does not do it justice—and search for whales. Linnea went on a ship once a week, turned on her microphone, and guided all the tourists through the adventure, while searching for whales or any other sea creatures to be spotted.

When Linnea told me that our trip would be highlighted by a whale watching tour, my excitement levels skyrocketed. I had never seen a whale before, unless we're talking the film *Free Willy*, which is amazing, I might add.

Let me paint you a picture. We loaded the boat, I shook the captain's hand, I received a tour of the ship, the engine puttered, and we were off. Filled with excitement and exhilaration of what was to come, I could barely contain myself. Standing at the nose of the boat, head cocked straight into the wind, taking in the blue ocean completely surrounding us, I was ready to see a whale.

An hour passed, and then it hit me: "What if we don't see a whale?"

Linnea affirmed the harsh reality that this was a possibility. There had been tours taken where people had not seen whales. I couldn't believe it. You mean to tell me they don't put trackers on these things? They aren't just wearing collars so we can click a button and have their exact location? I guess that's not exactly how it works.

Although I had received this information, Linnea seemed dauntlessly confident that we were going to see a whale. The expert whale watcher believed, so I decided if the one who knows all about whales can have hope, I can too.

Two hours passed. No whale. This is why I propose we change the name of "whale watching" to "whale waiting," because let's be honest, you aren't guaranteed watching—but you are guaranteed waiting.

Three hours passed and Linnea made the announcement, "We will be turning around soon. We will continue to keep our eyes open."

Hope was dwindling, but I remembered Linnea, the expert, and she still believed. That was it. I was going to believe, too. We were going to see a *Free Willy* that day.

One hour later, as the ship had already turned around, headed back to shore, the masses of tourists crowded to the front of the boat as if Taylor Swift was walking by. (I know Jesus can walk on water, but Taylor Swift can't, no matter how much you Swifties believe.)

Although it wasn't a famous pop star, you could not deny, something was happening. That "something" was one of the most beautiful natural sights of my life. I wish I could give the details of the type of whale and the size, but all I can tell you is I saw the biggest creature I've ever seen in my life surface above the water for at least five seconds. And I only saw the tail.

Linnea went into full nerd mode talking all about whales and their habitats. If only I was listening—the moment was too blissful for that. But I do remember her mentioning how they dive hundreds of feet deep into the water before coming back up. As if on cue, the whale re-surfaced right when Linnea said we should have expected it too.

We saw a whale. Multiple times. And it was so worth the wait.

There are many things in life that feel like "whale waiting." I have felt like I have been whale waiting for years for multiple things, and I have lost hope multiple times, almost to the point of convincing myself I will never receive what I'm waiting for. But then I remember that my true tour guide, Jesus, *The Spark Plug,* knows everything there is to know about his profession. He knows what he is doing, and he still has faith and belief that it's going to happen. In fact, he *knows* it's going to happen. And if I could trust Linnea, a whale watcher? Then I better be able to trust God, my father, who just wants me to believe in what I am waiting for.

Another word for belief in what is to come is "faith." Faith is believing even when we can't see. When Jesus arose from the dead and all of the disciples saw him except Thomas, Thomas said, "I won't believe it unless I see the wounds in his hands, put my fingers into them, and place my hand into the wounds in his side" (John 20:25b, NLT).

It wasn't until Thomas actually put his hands into the wounds on Jesus' side, when Jesus responded, "You believe because you have seen me. Blessed are those who believe without seeing me" (John 20:29, NLT).

Blessed are those who believe without seeing. Blessed are those who have faith. I firmly believe that God is a God who knows our hearts, our desires, and exactly what we need. He wants us to believe in him, and to believe that we will receive the blessings he has in store for us. I believe that with true faith, God will bless you with more than you can imagine, and he will give you many things you are waiting for—as long as they are in line with God's heart.

I can't sit here and guarantee that God will give you everything you might wait for on this earth. I can't say that he will show you every whale, even so much as a tail. But I can guarantee one thing, the absolutely one true thing worth waiting for. If you believe in your heart in what you can't see, if you accept him as your Lord and savior, you *will* receive the most important thing worth waiting for: heaven. And if that seems too far away, it really isn't. That is good news for us impatient people—you don't have to wait in order to experience heaven on this earth. A relationship with Jesus can happen right here, right now. No wait. No tricks. You can see the whale. You just have to accept him. And it is the most beautiful thing you can ever imagine—now and forever.

No matter what you're waiting for, here's my advice: board the ship, wait, and believe. Your guide believes. You probably should, too.

RIGHT HERE WITH RICHARD

August 28 to August 29, Vermont
Days 94 through 95

Leaving Linnea, I was able to visit my family in New York for some donuts and orange juice on the way to Vermont. It was great to be present and enjoy quality time with this part of my family, who I only get to see every few years. After a very nice hour with them, I was back on the beaten path.

I was headed to Vermont, where I had no one to stay with. Fortunately, at this point I had become a pro at making last-second plans and not worrying—unlike at the beginning of my trip, when I had extreme worry every time someone backed out. Now, when setbacks happened, I just shrugged my shoulders and figured it must have been God's plan.

Let's pause and hear the power in the statement above. I once worried so much about the future and what was next. Just two months later, in the same exact situation, I was not worried at all, because I knew God had a plan and I trusted him. Because God taught me a lesson, I learned the lesson, and I actually applied it to my life.

Now that I find myself at home, three years later, I often forget this lesson. I worry about "what's next" and forget the lesson that God taught me. Perhaps one of the most important lessons of this book is that God does amazing things in our lives. He speaks to us and teaches us lessons.

My biggest fault is that I forget what God has already taught me and I don't always apply his lessons to my life. I am learning how much easier it is to go with the grain, to go with God. When he teaches you something, he doesn't want you to have to learn it again. If you teach a dog to sit, they know how to sit forever. What I am learning is that God loves me like a puppy, but let's be honest: I am not a puppy anymore. He has already taught me how to sit, and if I want to make things a little easier on myself, I should probably listen.

Enough of that rant. It's germane, I promise, Your Honor.

So God taught me not to worry about what was next. Without worry, I opened up the Airbnb app and found a rustic cabin in Castleton, Vermont. What I didn't know about this cabin was that I would be greeted by a sweet, old, English man named Richard. Richard greeted me, pointed me toward my bedroom, gave me a tour of the beautiful back deck that showed hundreds of miles of ginormous evergreen trees, warned me of the black bears in the area, then left me there alone.

Without any plan, I decided a hike in this part of the country was absolutely necessary. After taking in the historic Hubbardton Battlefield, I found myself at Taconic Ramble State Park. I was in the early stages of training for a marathon, so there was only one choice here: a trail run. Trail runs are always majestic, exploring so much beauty and newness all at once. You aren't running on a track with the same static sights; you are running through a forest of shrubbery—hopping, leaping, and skipping over the different terrain.

One mile in, I reached the top of the hike. There was a beautiful lookout point nearby that I knew I needed to enjoy after my run. The only problem was that I planned to run one-and-a-half miles. With only half a mile left, I didn't want to run much further away from the stunning lookout point—so I did something that I would not recommend in real life: I started running on the same path of the hike, back and forth, back and forth, back and forth—for half a mile. I ran around two hundred feet, turned around, and did it again, repeatedly, until finally reaching my one-and-a-half miles. The final half mile was repetitive, to say the least. The only good thing about this plan was where I ended: the most beautiful lookout point I could find. I was then able to sit still, enjoy where I was, and be immersed in all the beauty around me.

Right now in life, I am waiting for a wife, I am waiting for career discernment, I am waiting for Jeff Probst from CBS's *Survivor* to call me. Sometimes I find myself forgetting the lesson God has already taught me: do not worry about what is next. Trust God.

Sometimes I feel like I am running back and forth, back and forth, back and forth, waiting for the next thing, when God already has me at a beautiful lookout point. God has me in a job I never thought I'd be in, being able to disciple people I never would have otherwise met. God has me helping plant a church, being discipled and mentored by a great friend, writing a book that I pray makes ripples in his Kingdom. God has me exactly where I need to be. I just need to sit still, enjoy where I am, and be present for the beauty around me.

Don't get me wrong—sitting still doesn't mean not planning, or doing nothing and expecting something to come your way. *Do not waste your waiting.* This road trip didn't happen by waiting and doing nothing. This book didn't magically appear. Seek out opportunities, prepare yourself for what you are waiting for, pray, and be productive in your waiting. But in all of that, don't forget where you are: at a beautiful lookout.

Later that night, I sat down at the kitchen counter and had a talk with Richard. I had the next day for New Hampshire planned, I was interviewing for jobs the next few days—I was being productive in my waiting. But I didn't let it take me away from where I was: with Richard. Richard was fascinated and intrigued by my story and was happy to share stories of other fascinating people who had ventured through his neck of the woods.

There was joy in the conversation. An old, wise man and a young, inspired man. Together, I think they could conquer the world. In that conversation, I felt it—the peace. In that moment, right there with Richard, I was exactly where I was supposed to be.

Waiting is hard. It can make your head spin and make you want to run in every direction, but it can really be quite simple. Be obedient where God has you waiting. If it's with your family, on a beautiful hike, managing a gas station, single, or sipping coffee with an old Brit, sit still, enjoy where you are, and be present. You are where you are supposed to be right now. These moments don't come back, the "next" will come, and *The Spark Plug* already has it figured out.

The wait is beautiful. The lessons in the waiting are limitless. Gratitude and fulfillment. Patience and obedience. Faith and trust.

Being present. It's all in the waiting, and it's all in Jesus. I encourage you, whatever you're waiting for at this moment, to remember that *The Spark Plug* is with you. Take a deep breath.

Inhale. Exhale.

Inhale. Exhale.

The Spark Plug is with you. I hope you and he enjoy your wait together.

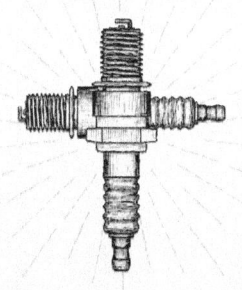

Not What,
But Who

The last part of this once-in-a-lifetime adventure flew by. I visited fourteen states in the final twenty-one days. Six of those final fourteen states were special. Let me tell you why.

SIGI

September 4 to September 5, 2021 - Pennsylvania
Days 101 through 102

Sigi was my "college mom." The very first day of freshman year, Sigi was the first person I met. My curly haired friend, who was a junior at the time, welcomed me with a sweet giggle and wondrous smile that was so accepting and kind. At the time, I didn't think Sigi would become a friend of mine, in all honesty. Sigi, short for Siglinde, wasn't the "typical" friend I had back in high school. She was different—different in that she was herself, and not afraid to be that.

It wasn't until a few months later I realized Sigi was in my life to stay. She was a Resident Assistant on my floor, and before I knew it, I had found a new best friend to add to my list of amazing people in my life. Staying up late in the commons showing her my country music at 3 a.m., having real life conversations, and just being goofy together became routine. I don't know what I would have done without my college mom. She was always there for me, always so kind and loving, and I know if I called her today, she would be here in a heartbeat.

When I was exiting the Northeast, I knew I had to reach out to Sigi, as she was now living in Philadelphia. There was no doubt that she would host me for a night in her apartment, and that's all it was. One night. I showed up at 8 p.m. I waited for Sigi to get off of work, then we spent hours talking, catching up, and reminiscing on her living room couch. I didn't care what we did that night; I was just blessed to be in the presence of my friend.

RENEE

September 8 to September 10, 2021 - Illinois, Wisconsin
Days 105 through 107

Renee is my brother-in-law's mother. I have known her for the better half of a decade. She has always been kind to me, whether donating to any fundraisers I have been a part of, being a surefire comment on all my Facebook posts, or treating me like a son whenever she visits my sister and her husband.

Renee was more than happy to extend an invite to help me in Illinois, where she resides, and Wisconsin. The only reason that I wanted to go to Wisconsin was 1) to say that I had spent time in Wisconsin, and 2) to purchase my shot glass, sticker, and postcard.

Renee and I drove hours north into Wisconsin until we finally found the perfect place: The Mars Cheese Castle. Not only home to a lot of cheese, but also shot glasses, stickers, and postcards. After my friend and I ate lunch in Kenosha, we headed back to Illinois.

In Illinois—more specifically, in her backyard—we golfed nine holes and followed it up with a great dinner and a beer. There really wasn't much else to the trip. No crazy story to tell. The story is mundane. The story is about spending time with someone who I was very thankful for and comfortable with. It didn't matter what we did; I was just thankful to be spending time with Renee.

ALYJO

August 13 to August 14, 2021 - Minnesota
Days 110 through 111

Alyjo, better known as Alex, is someone I formed a crush on years ago over social media. After sliding into her DMs and being very persistent, I received a date. And then another. One problem: she lived in Minneapolis and I lived in South Dakota. Agreeing not to pursue anything romantically, we remained friends over the years, to the point that she was willing to host me in Minnesota on my way home.

Alex and I had a very relaxed night together. We went to a local brewery, tasted a flight of ciders, and played some of the most underrated games out there: Jenga and Battleship. Soaking up our ciders with pizza, we enjoyed a fun night full of conversation and laughter.

Again, not a crazy story here. The next morning, I went to the Mall of America and then was on my way. Nothing special, just a night out with an old friend. But to me, it was special. Jenga or Battleship, it didn't matter. Spending time with Alex was special.

KOVS AND REECE

August 10 to August 13, 2021 - Iowa, Missouri
Days 107 through 110

Luke (otherwise known as "Kovs") and I became friends in eighth grade. One fateful day, we were walking after school in a similar direction and started talking. The conversation led to me convincing my older sister to give him a ride home once we got to the Toyota—yes, the same Toyota that I made the trip in. That day sealed a friendship that is still alive and well, fourteen years later. So alive and well that although he lives hundreds of miles from me, last month we were able to enjoy "emo night" together—a tradition we created four years ago.

Reece and I didn't become friends until our freshman year of high school when we happened to be in the same biology class together. Reece was very quiet, and he still is. The only thing that sparked our friendship was our common interest in sports. When I saw Reece wearing a Yankees jersey one day in the hallway and a Cincinnati Reds shirt later on, being the baseball fanatic I am, I had to spark a convo. Reece moved away to Texas after the first semester of freshman year. I fully expected the friendship to fade, but Reece texted me a month after moving about—what? Sports. Our shared interest sparked a conversation that is still ongoing. That's right, a text message exchange has been back and forth for thirteen years. I have been blessed to see Reece a handful of times since 2010, and continue to grow our friendship in person.

Reece, Kovs, and I have been in an ongoing group text together since high school, but there have only been a few times that we have all three been in the same city at once. Off the top of my head, I believe it has happened three times since we were freshman in high school.

During the trip, Reece was living with his family for the summer while searching for pharmaceutical jobs in Des Moines, Iowa. Kovs was attending medical school, also in Des Moines. There was no better place to stop. The three of us were able to enjoy a dinner together in reunion, enjoying a moment that we rarely ever get.

For the next few days, Reece's family graciously hosted me. Those days were spent driving to Kansas City, Missouri to buy my souvenirs, watching the legendary *Kicking and Screaming movie* with Will Ferrill, and supporting Reece's seven-year-old sister, Emma, at her extremely non-competitive soccer game. Although we didn't do anything too noteworthy, we spent time together. And that's all that I really wanted.

JESUS

I have known Jesus for almost four years. I have known about him for much longer, but I have only truly known him, in my heart, for a short time.

In the last four years I have done many things with Jesus by my side. I have worked in schools, coached high school baseball, coached college softball, and managed a convenience store. I have led multiple Bible studies and helped plant a church. I have run a marathon, jumped out of an airplane, and traveled the whole country. I've done a lot.

There are also plenty of times where I feel like I'm not doing enough, or maybe I don't love doing what I'm doing right now. That's only because I start doing it alone. I often forget that *God is with me everywhere I go.*

It's like when Reece and I drove to Missouri for hours to get my shot glass and souvenirs. He was quiet, and I sometimes forgot he was riding shotgun. He was there, but sometimes I forgot about his presence because I wasn't focused on him. While he was still and quiet, just hanging with his friend, I forgot him, even though he was always there.

I forget how much Jesus loves me and how much he has impacted my life. I forget that Jesus is one of my best friends—he is with me wherever I go. And if he truly is with me wherever I go, why can't I just enjoy every moment with him, like I did with Sigi, Renee, Alex, Kovs, and Reece? It doesn't matter what you do. It's about who you do it with.

Whatever you are doing, Jesus is with you wherever you go.

"I am with you always, even to the end of the age" (Matthew 28:20b, NLT).

Think about the person who means the most to you. Think about the last time you spent time together. Was it overwhelmingly exciting? How about the last five times? I'm guessing there was a bit of underwhelmingness in there, *but*, did you enjoy almost every moment in their presence? Probably so.

Time with Jesus can be the same. He's a best friend who wants to do extreme things with you—go to the concerts and jump out of planes. But he also wants to go to work and sit in your car with you. Highs, lows, extremes, mundanes, whatever it may be—Jesus is with you.

"Then you will experience God's peace, which exceeds anything we can understand. His peace will guard your hearts and minds as you live in Christ Jesus" (Philippians 4:7, NLT).

The scripture above references God's peace when we go to him in prayer. But it's also referring to his peace that is generally available, a peace we cannot understand which will guard our hearts and minds as we live in Christ and he lives in us.

Christ is in us. He is wherever we go, and, might I remind you, it doesn't matter what you do, but who you are doing it with. Living out your dream job or managing a gas station. Traveling the country or having never left your small town. Attending church or working out. On a walk or on your couch. Wherever you go, whatever you do, you do it with *The Spark Plug*. He's already there.

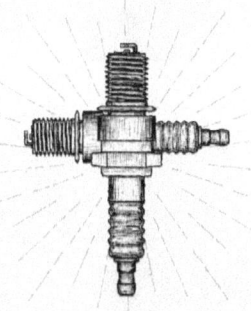

THE SPARK PLUG

June 4 - June June 8, 2021 - Utah

Days 9-13

Remember I said I experienced more than one miracle in Utah? Keep reading.

Seven days into my trip, I left Denver, Colorado and headed towards Provo, Utah. On a high from my amazing time in Colorado, I couldn't stop smiling on my seven-hour drive through the beautiful mountains and canyons. Nothing was going to deter me. Nothing.

Three hours away from Provo, my 2010 Toyota Corolla with 242,000 miles began to putter. My anxious right foot hit the accelerator and the car only continued to decrease in speed. I pulled over to the shoulder, beautiful desert all around me. My car had broken down in the middle of nowhere—but I wasn't worried. Instead, I felt the most uncanny feeling ever: an overwhelming peace that exceeded anything I could understand. My car broke down, but I just knew everything was going to be okay. It was as if this was part of God's glorious plan.

After calling my mom and dad and turning the key multiple times, my reliable old Toyota decided to kick back on. With three hours to go, I knew there could be a very interesting journey ahead.

Sixty minutes later, while speeding on the highway with the mountains on my left and a steep drop leading to a rushing river to my right, sure enough—my car had nothing left. I pulled over to the minimal shoulder on the right side of the highway.

Step One: call someone.

Step One, however, was denied. I had absolutely no cell phone service. I couldn't even send a text message without the "message failed" receipt.

Step Two: pop the hood and check it out.

Step Two was also denied. I know absolutely nothing about cars, and nothing even looked remotely "weird" to me.

I was stuck. In the middle of nowhere. No cell phone service. The sun was setting, and I was still two hours away from my destination. My map app couldn't pull anything up to show me the nearest town to walk to. I had no clue what to do. I had no one to call on.

But then, I remembered that I did.

Step Three: pray to God.

Step Three was approved. Within five minutes of praying, a car pulled up right behind me and a man asked me what was wrong with my car. I told the gentleman I had absolutely no clue what was wrong, and he saved me: "Need a ride?"

What other option did I have? My new acquaintance, Conrad, told me to hop on in. Grabbing my necessities—my pocket knife for safety, my phone, and my keys—I did just that.

Without any cell phone service, I was unable to tell anyone in my family anything about what had happened. My only hope was that this man was not going to kill me. The next two hours felt like ten minutes.

Sure enough, *The Spark Plug,* Jesus, entered the conversation. He was Mormon, and we began talking about the differences in our faith and beliefs. As we approached Chick-Fil-A, God's chicken,

I shared my story—well, not my story. God's story. How he took me from someone who was depressed, hopeless, and searching desperately for anything to give him life, to someone set free, full of faith and hope, and completely and wholly found. This was God's story of how he changed my life.

Sure enough, the story hit Conrad like a piercing sword, as he related very much to my struggles I had before Jesus. As he dropped me off at Callie's doorstep in Provo, we prayed together, then said our goodbyes.

Callie and I called insurance. We called the tow truck company. We did all the things. Within three hours, we met the tow truck back at my car. It was 11 p.m. The next three to four days were full of two things: exploring and worrying.

I was in the stormy middle of God's amazing plan, but I couldn't see it. As we drove across Utah, seeing all the beautiful National Parks, I couldn't help but wonder in the back of my head if my trip was over. Was my car done for? Was it fixable, but too costly? Was I about to head back home only seven days into my trip? The worries now started to flood my mind and pessimistic thoughts were winning. I was questioning whether this was a sign from God to move straight to Colorado—a place I had just fallen in love with. I was prepared to end the trip.

The day before I was supposed to continue on to Boise, Idaho, I received a call from the mechanic. The initial diagnosis: the catalytic converter was not in good shape. I didn't know what this meant other than I would be footing a large repair bill. Discouraged, thinking there was no way my car was going to make it through the next four months, I was losing faith. Maybe this trip wasn't what God had planned for me, after all.

The next morning, my final day in Utah, the tow shop told us the car was ready. Not sure what damage was done, I walked in with an uneasy heart, ready for it to be ripped out of my chest.

"The spark plugs is all it was. We just had to replace the spark plugs."

With a bill under $300, I was told my Corolla was ready to go. I was amazed. Every day that I look back, I become more and more amazed. My car broke down in the middle of nowhere with no help, yet help arrived. My car, with 242,000 miles on it, just needed a quick fix, and I had the "green light" to proceed on the four-month trek. My trip wasn't delayed one minute. None of this made sense.

But God doesn't always make sense.

If the spark plugs hadn't been replaced, the remainder of this trip never would have happened. Not even that, my car never would have run again. Spark plugs aren't just helpful to the life and functionality of the car, they are absolutely, 100 percent necessary. The spark plugs are life.

The Spark Plug, Jesus, is life. *The Spark Plug* is not just important, but absolutely necessary. *The Spark Plug* is everything.

Road trips are parallel to life. There are many twists and turns. There are hectic storms and amazing sunsets. There are roadblocks and expressways. Road trips are unpredictable, and that is what makes them so great and unforgettable.

The one necessary thing for a road trip is a functioning vehicle, and what is absolutely necessary for a functioning vehicle?

The spark plugs.

Here is what I have come to conclude: To travel, we need *The Spark Plug.* But what else? The driver. Someone to turn the keys, to ignite the engine so *The Spark Plug* can do its job and keep moving the car forward. Even with *The Spark Plug,* if you never turn the key and hit the gas, the car won't move.

Are you on the road trip I call life? Let me give you some advice. Turn the key, start the engine, and let *The Spark Plug* move you forward. Let him take over and guide you down the road. The pace is up to you, but he is there, every step of the way, igniting.

Maybe you know *The Spark Plug*. Maybe you don't. But I promise you, with the true, real, *Spark Plug*—with Jesus, my friend, this is only the beginning.

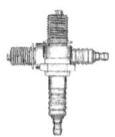

STEPHEN'S STATE-BY-STATE BULLET POINTS FROM HIS POSTCARDS

1. South Dakota
   a. Joshua 1:9.
2. Nebraska
   a. Take chances: risk it to get the biscuit.
3. Kansas
   a. Be yourself.
4. Colorado
   a. God is always working.
5. Utah
   a. Be patient.
6. Idaho
   a. Not all things go to plan.
   b. Lead, even if it is uncomfortable.
7. Montana
   a. We may waver, but God never does.
8. Wyoming
   a. Life is hard. We need an anchor: God.

9. Washington
    a. God will provide.
    b. Do not worry.
10. Oregon
    a. Alone and quiet time is important.
11. Nevada
    a. It's hard to think and act like Jesus.
    b. We are all so different in our unique ways.
12. California
    a. Rest is necessary.
13. Arizona
    a. People are craving something—it's Jesus, they just don't know it yet.
14. New Mexico
    a. God creates beautiful sunsets, and he created you.
15. Oklahoma
    a. Quiet time outdoors is great.
16. Arkansas
    a. The world is angry. Try to spread some love in it.
    b. Nothing is easy, but everything is better with God.
17. Texas
    a. Love your mom.
18. Mississippi
    a. Enjoy every moment with loved ones.
19. Louisiana
    a. Be nice to your mom.
20. Alabama
    a. A lot of things go unplanned. Ride the wave—trust God.
21. Tennessee
    a. Keep going.

22. Georgia
    a. Go with your gut.
23. South Carolina
    a. Family.
    b. God will do things in ways you don't expect.
24. Florida
    a. Trust God and do not doubt him.
25. North Carolina
    a. Run in the rain.
26. West Virginia
    a. Let your thoughts and feelings depend on who the Lord
        says you are—not others.
27. Kentucky
    a. Don't sulk. Call someone who will make you laugh.
    b. Don't overthink.
28. Virginia
    a. Trust the Lord's plan.
29. Maryland
    a. Put God in the center of everything.
30. Delaware
    a. God always shows up.
31. New Jersey
    a. Love the Lord first.
32. Long Island
    a. God is molding you.
33. Vermont
    a. Meet new people.
34. New Hampshire
    a. Exploring alone is fun.
    b. Take the cool-looking exit.

35. Maine
    a. Sometimes you're supposed to reach someone unexpected.
36. Connecticut
    a. There is beauty in the little things; let your hand surf outside the car window.
37. Rhode Island
    a. Always jump in the ocean.
38. Massachusetts
    a. Love is way deeper than the superficial stuff.
39. Pennsylvania
    a. Reminiscing with an old friend is fun.
40. Ohio
    a. Always enjoy every moment.
41. Michigan
    a. God inserts himself.
42. Illinois
    a. Try new things.
43. Wisconsin
    a. So many people are there for you.
44. Iowa
    a. True friendship will always pick up where it left off.
45. Missouri
    a. Love everyone, no matter what.
46. Minnesota
    a. Search within a person's heart.
47. North Dakota
    a. The end is bittersweet.
48. Indiana
    a. Live life to the fullest.

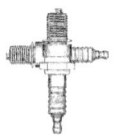

ABOUT THE AUTHOR

Oswald's four mantras are: "live life to the fullest," "through God for God," "risk it to get the biscuit," and "weird and awkward." He fully believes in squeezing every ounce out of life with God at the forefront, taking chances, and being his true, goofy self.

Jumping out of an airplane, running a marathon on his own with minimal training, writing this book, exploring God's creation with strangers, or mentoring people through sport are just a few of the things Oswald has done that make him feel he is living out his mantras.

Oswald has degrees from the University of Indianapolis and Mount Marty University in sport management, business, and coaching leadership. He doesn't use them at all, yet he uses them everyday.

Oswald loves people and loves Jesus.

He would love to hear from you about how this book worked in your life.

Email him at: thesparkplugbook@gmail.com

WAIT! I NEED YOU!

Thank you so much for reading my book. I pray that God used this book to speak to you and spark something in you.

I would love to hear your feedback and see what your thoughts are on *The Spark Plug*.

You've made it this far. Please take two minutes right now to leave a helpful review on Amazon letting me know what you thought of the book.

This is very helpful and appreciated. Thank you so much!

—Stephen John Oswald Jr.

CITATIONS

1. "Why Are Spark Plugs so Important to Your Engine?" Christian Brothers Automotive, May 21, 2019. https://www.cbac. com/media-center/blog/2019/may/why-are-spark-plugs-so-important-to-your-engine-/#:~:text=Your%20spark%20 plugs%20are%20what%20supply%20the%20spark,that%20 electricity%20can%20jump%20the%20gap%20between%20 them.

2. Merriam-Webster.com Dictionary, s.v. "miracle," accessed July 31, 2024, https://www.merriam-webster.com/dictionary/ miracle.

3. Scripture quotations are taken from the Holy Bible, New Living Translation, copyright © 1996, 2004, 2015 by Tyndale House Foundation. Used by permission of Tyndale House Publishers, Carol Stream, Illinois 60188. All rights reserved.

www.ingramcontent.com/pod-product-compliance
Lightning Source LLC
Chambersburg PA
CBHW021142130626
46554CB00005B/1623

*9 7 9 8 8 9 3 1 6 7 3 5 1 *